For God's Sake, Grow Up!

A Call to Spiritual Maturity

David Ravenhill

D1113266

Destiny Image® Publishers, Inc.
P.O. Box 310
Shippensburg, PA 17257-0310

"Speaking to the Purposes of God for This Generation
and for the Generations to Come"

ISBN 1-56043-299-3

For Worldwide Distribution
Printed in the U.S.A.

Sixth Printing: 2000   Seventh Printing: 2001

This book and all other Destiny Image, Revival Press, Mercy Place, Fresh Bread, Destiny Image Fiction, and Treasure House books are available at Christian bookstores and distributors worldwide.

For a U.S. bookstore nearest you, call **1-800-722-6774**.
For more information on foreign distributors, call **717-532-3040**.
Or reach us on the Internet: **www.reapernet.com**

Dedication

To my precious wife Nancy, for her loving and loyal support over the past 33 years of marriage and ministry together. She alone knows the pressure and pleasure of serving God with me. Our ministry has uprooted us numerous times. We have lived in several different countries for extended periods of time, and yet with all the changes, she has willingly followed, and unpacked and set up another home. Thanks, Darling, I love you.

To our three wonderful daughters: Lisa, Tina, and Debra. Life would not have been the same without you. I love you more than words can tell. To our son-in-law, George Reninger, Tina's husband, and our two grandchildren, Micah and Lilly, thanks for enriching our family—you guys are great.

Finally, to my parents, no amount of money can purchase a godly heritage. Proverbs states that "A good name is better than riches." How grateful I am to God for the privilege of being raised in a godly family. I never recall a day that my mother wasn't at home tirelessly serving the family she loved—rightly she was named Martha. Leonard, my father, is now with the

Master he worshiped and served. As he lay dying at the age of 87, after 70 years of ministry, I sat with my mother at his bedside in the hospital. I reflected on the example of his life on a small scrap of paper where I began to write the following tribute:

Tribute to a Godly Dad

I knew a man who gave his life,
To see revival fire,
He prayed by day, he prayed by night,
To birth this one desire.

He had but one obsession,
To see a glorious bride,
Arrayed in spotless purity,
Brought to her bridegroom's side.

His power while in the pulpit,
Was matched by very few,
And yet, he loved the closet—
There with the God he knew.

While others strove for man's applause,
For fortune and for fame,
He had but one ambition,
To exalt his Master's name.

For eighty-seven years,
He lived just for eternity,
A man of faith and wisdom
And true humility.

He knew one day he'd have to stand,
Before God's Judgment Seat,
And so he ran to win the prize,
His mission to complete.

The fortune that he left behind,
Was not in stocks or gold,
But lives transformed and challenged—
Their stories yet untold.

There is no greater privilege,
Than this that I have had,
Of knowing this great man of God,
And having him as Dad.

In the words of the Psalmist, "The lines have fallen to me in the best places. For this inheritance of mine is the best for me" (Ps. 16:6, Septuagint version). To God alone be the glory.

Acknowledgments

How I would love to take this finished manuscript and go back in time to one of my many English teachers and show her that she had made a major mistake in failing to recognize my true giftedness.

Unfortunately, this book is not the product of my own ability or talent. Most of the credit goes to the unsung heroes who have worked behind the scenes, laboring long hours to correct, adjust, and in many cases, rewrite much of the material.

I'm first of all indebted to my mother who painstakingly sat with me night after night during my senior years of school, encouraging me to keep going despite my longing to call it quits and my believing that God had not gifted me with acumen in the academic realm.

Since those years, God has graciously given me Nancy, my wife, who has the unique ability to smell a grammatical error a mile away. What a gift, what a treasure.

The work on this book began in Christchurch, New Zealand, in 1987, thanks to the help of Alan and Ann Ferguson who transferred much of my early draft onto a computer, a contraption I still find I have nothing whatsoever in common with and to this day it still remains a mystery.

I would also like to express my deep appreciation to Brad and Estelle Jackson for their valuable time and work in editing the original manuscript. Their labor of love will be rewarded on that Great Day.

My thanks also to Steve Lambert for the major part he played in revamping the first manuscript. Steve's gifting will soon be evident to the Christian community as he is presently working on several books that are soon to be released.

My gratitude to Judy Doyle for her rare literary skill and creative genius. Without her help I'm sure this book would have never seen the light of day.

My love and appreciation to my beloved father (now in his heavenly home) who so faithfully prayed for me over the past 50 years. Only eternity will reveal the hours of intercession he spent on my behalf. There is no greater earthly reward than the example of a godly life—thanks, Dad.

Finally, to the Lord Himself who has chosen this weak vessel to be a laborer together with Him. There is no calling higher, no privilege greater than serving and ministering with Him, for Him, and to Him. To Him alone be all the glory!

Contents

Preface

We might as well face it: If the Church could be compared to an airline, many customers would hesitate to fly. Our standards are low; our safety record is dismal. We allow almost anyone in the cockpit, whether or not he or she is qualified.

When these "pilots" are forced to ditch their planes, unfortunately, it's usually the passengers who suffer the most. Some manage to walk away with minor problems. Others join the growing list of victims who never recover from their injuries.

Called, Conformed, Commissioned

The leadership qualifications listed in First Timothy 3 for bishops, deacons, and their families seem to have little to do with the fact that an individual has a "calling" to fly. The divine calling and gifting of God are, of course, essential but, alone, they are insufficient. We can destroy with an immature, undeveloped character the very ministry we built with our gifts and calling. Without character, ultimately we self-destruct.

All too often we hear of spiritual leaders who, though claiming to be filled with the Spirit of God, had to step down due to marital unfaithfulness, financial wrongdoing, or some other ethical failure. Why? One of the major mistakes in the Church today has been the exaltation of natural abilities and spiritual gifts at the expense of godly character.

By "character" I mean conformity to Christ's image. You see, the Greek word *charakter* is derived from the word *die* as in minting. It carries the thought of image, coinage, copy, or likeness. God is particular about whom He chooses. He is looking for men and women of maturity and beauty of character.

God first begins by *calling*: "Come, follow Me… " Then He continues with His *conforming*: "…And I will make you." He ends with His *commissioning*: "Go ye." However, many mistake His calling for His commissioning.

For example, as a young man, Moses knew the calling of God: "he supposed that his brethren understood that God was granting them deliverance through him; but they did not understand" (Acts 7:25). It wasn't until some 40 years had passed, during which time God was working to "conform" Moses, that he was commissioned.

Similarly, Jesus, as a young boy, knew His *calling* was to be about His Father's business. During the ensuing years, He grew in wisdom and stature, and in favor with God and man—His *conforming*. Then at the age of 30, Jesus was *commissioned* by the Father: The Spirit of God was sent to rest upon Him.

Calling is not enough. Commissioning is not enough. We must be conformed to the image of Christ.

Our heavenly Father's goal is that:

*…We all come to the unity of the faith and the knowledge of the Son of God, to a perfect man, to the measure of the stature of the fullness of Christ; **that we should no longer***

be children, tossed to and fro and carried about with every wind of doctrine, by the trickery of men, in the cunning craftiness of deceitful plotting, but, speaking the truth in love, may grow up in all things into Him who is the head—Christ—from whom the whole body, joined and knit together by what every joint supplies, according to the effective working by which every part does its share, causes growth of the body for the edifying of itself in love (Ephesians 4:13-16 NKJ, emphasis mine).

Unless we are also conformed to the image of Christ, *unless we grow up*, our lives and labors for the Lord will be incomplete and disappointing in the light of eternity.

Key Issues Confronting the Church Today

This book wasn't designed to be a complete or comprehensive manual on Christian maturity. Neither was it designed strictly for persons behind the pulpit, for all believers are called to do the work of the ministry. Rather, I've divided the book into three sections focusing on what I believe to be some of the key issues facing the individual believer and the Church as a whole in our day.

The first section, *Laying a Firm Foundation*, provides instruction on growing in God, understanding and serving God's purpose, increasing our desire for God, learning the fear of the Lord, and conforming to His character.

The second section, *Preparing for Ministry*, examines several vital principles that need to be operating in a believer's life before he or she is fully equipped to step out in ministry, for Scripture indicates that leaders carry not only increased responsibility, but also increased accountability. Therefore, this section examines the moral and spiritual requirements for leadership, gleaning lessons from the lives of leaders such as Moses, Joshua, Abraham, and David. We also examine our privileges and responsibilities as kings and priests.

The final section, *Fulfilling Your Vision*, describes how we're to function as mature saints, participating in both sacrifice and service in God's royal priesthood through intercession, celebration, and proclamation. Here, we confront the ongoing battle between good and evil in the spiritual realm. We see the necessity of waging spiritual warfare.

Our Challenge

These are serious times. God's Church must be mature. It must be prepared and equipped. The Lord is sending out a summons even now for believers to enroll in His school of the Spirit. The summer of our childhood is over. It's time to take our places at His feet, open the tablets of our hearts, and say: "Speak, Lord, for Thy servant heareth." It's time to grow up.

Introduction

Many present-day Christians seem to have experienced three stages: condemnation, salvation, and stagnation.

Babyhood is a delightful thing; perpetual babyhood is deplorable. The *perpetual* spiritual infant is an embarrassment to God. God wants us rich in spiritual things. Unless we are grown-up in Christ, we will be a liability—childish and petty, wanting attention all the time, and wanting to be amused. For years, a church in the Southeast has sent me its bulletin. It's a pathetic thing. No doubt its "full program" is considered, "Christian activity"; but I shudder when there are weekly classes in ceramics and painting, skating parties, and a host of infantile things that most country clubs would shun. A church like this will never, never be on the devil's danger list.

No church group that knows spiritual warfare has wiener roasts or even passion plays. There is a *real* warfare. I have said before that we are an arrogant, self-styled bunch of believers. We "believe" to the point of inconvenience—and then quit.

We know by inspiration and by participation that Job was right when he said, "Man was born unto trouble, as the sparks fly upward." Man is also born to choices, decisions, and options.

Decide now! "Choose you this day." This text in its original framework is familiar to most of us: Joshua had a dramatic confrontation with Israel. They could serve the gods their fathers served before the flood, or the local gods of the Amorites with whom they were then living, *or* they could staunchly stand with Joshua who said, "As for me and my house, we will serve the Lord."

But let's put the emphasis here: "Choose—*this day*." I made a choice, maybe years ago, to follow the Lamb withersoever He goeth. That's fine, but *this day* I am challenged to follow "other gods." Vanity may be one of them; emulation may be another. Laziness could have dominion over me unless I am living with "eternity's values in view." Covetousness is a beguiling god. It calls itself by other names—usually its mask is "success" or just plain "getting on." Nevertheless, it will steal this day unless I unmask this deceiver. This day will never come again. There is no market where one can buy old days or partly worn-out days. They come and go, for better, for worse. There is a sense in which I am the master of my fate, I am the captain of my soul.

Slave of time I may be, but there never yet was a master who could enslave the spirit. I can be prison bound, yet be free. I can be crippled, and yet be a spiritual athlete overcoming hurdles others fall at. I can choose this day to pray or not to pray, to fast or not to fast, to speak generously or critically of others. This day I can repair some damage to a brother's reputation or further foul it up. Today I can lay at His blessed feet tributes of worship and praise long overdue. Yesterday's choices are gone, tomorrow's are unborn. This is the day.

Leonard Ravenhill
Excerpted from Chapter 2, "Growing Out of Spiritual Infancy"
Revival God's Way, (Bethany House, 1983). Used with Permission.

Section One

Laying a Firm Foundation

Chapter One

Putting Away
Childish Things

Helen and Gilbert Doyle, a middle-aged Christian couple who had already taken over 50 foster children into their home through the years, in addition to rearing three children of their own, were overjoyed when a social services worker phoned with an unusual request. "How would you like to take care of a premature baby boy for us? His 16-year-old mother was only six months along in the pregnancy when he was born, and he weighed just two pounds at birth. He's up to four pounds now, and the doctor feels the baby needs to get out of the incubator and into some loving arms. How about it? Will you take him?"

Soon the little baby with the tiny turned-up nose and beautiful blue eyes had a home. In the weeks ahead, while Gilbert, a farmer, worked in his fields, Helen fed and rocked the baby and prayed hundreds of prayers over him. Whenever Gilbert came in, he took over the rocking while Helen straightened the house, got a load of washing done, and cooked a hot meal.

One morning after the baby had been in their home about six weeks, his eyes rolled back in his head and he made several strange "uhhhh, uhhhh, uhhhh" sounds. Then he passed out, remaining unconscious for two or three minutes. Helen raced to the phone and called the doctor. In less than an hour, she was sitting in his office.

"Doctor," she asked, "while you're examining the baby, would you mind checking his eyes? Something's not quite right."

A few minutes later, as the doctor placed the baby in Helen's arms, he smiled reassuringly. "The baby's eyes are fine, and I couldn't find anything else wrong, either. I just hope it's not epilepsy."

Four weeks later, when the baby passed out again, the doctor instructed the couple to take him to a pediatrician in a larger city nearby.

While the pediatrician was thoroughly going over the baby, Helen asked if he would mind checking his eyes.

"What makes you think there's anything wrong with the baby's eyes?" he asked. "They certainly appear to be normal, don't they?"

"Yes, they do. But something's just not right, Doctor. Would you examine them real good for me?"

After shining a tiny light in the baby's eyes, without saying a word, the doctor pushed a buzzer and another physician walked in. Turning to the anxious couple, the pediatrician asked, "Would you mind leaving the room while we conduct another test or two?"

After 15 minutes or so had passed, the doctor called Helen and Gilbert back into the examining room. "You were right," he sighed. "The baby is blind. I just hope he doesn't have what I think he has. We'd better admit him to the hospital three or four days for extensive tests. I want to monitor every drop of urine this baby passes."

Two days later, Gilbert stopped the doctor as he made his rounds. "Can you tell Helen and me what's wrong? What do you think the baby has?"

"As a matter of fact, I was on my way to give you the test results when you met me just now in the hall. I'm sorry to have to tell you this, but tests have confirmed that the baby has Lowe's syndrome, a hereditary condition in males characterized by growth retardation, mental retardation, hypotonia (lack of muscle tone), bilateral congenital cataracts, and glaucoma. A defect in the baby's kidneys results in impaired retention of various amino acids and salts."

Seeing the couple's blank stares, the doctor paused. "In other words, the kidneys work just the opposite of the way they're supposed to and literally poison the body by sending the *bad* back into the system while sending the *good* out."

The doctor paused again, leaning over and stroking the baby's soft cheek, as if gathering courage for what he was about to have to say. Then, clearing his throat, he continued.

"The condition has already made the baby blind, except for a tiny rim of light over the top of the cataracts on his eyes. It will eventually affect the brain, causing retardation, and it will affect his muscles. It will become increasingly difficult for the baby to swallow or to lift his arms and legs. His life expectancy is limited, and he will never grow beyond the size of an infant or toddler. I'm sorry. Very sorry."

Helen and Gilbert took the baby back home. With each passing month, he required more and more care, until finally the demands were constant. Either Helen or Gilbert had to hold him all the time, day and night. The baby barely moved his arms or legs, and then he couldn't lift them at all. All he could digest was milk, water, or juice. Because of his difficulty swallowing, he could take only an ounce or so at a time. Then he would have to stop and rest.

During the last week or so of his life, the baby's muscles had deteriorated so badly, he breathed in shallow gasps from the upper part of his lungs, and he had to be fed with an eyedropper since he could no longer suck a bottle. At seven months, he weighed only eight and a half pounds. Then he took pneumonia.

Helen was standing in the hospital beside the baby's incubator when he gave one final gasp, then he was gone.

With permission from the hospital personnel, the couple collected the baby's things, wrapped him in a blanket, and Helen held him in her arms, weeping and praying softly, as Gilbert drove the 35 miles back to the country town where they lived.

After pulling their car into the mortuary parking lot, Gilbert held out his hands and whispered, "Here, Helen. Let me carry him in." That tough, weather-beaten farmer held the baby all the time he and Helen made the funeral arrangements. Then, gently placing the child in the mortician's arms, he turned and literally ran to the car.

I can hardly tell that story without tears welling in my eyes. One reason is because I know that couple's grown son and daughter-in-law, and our friendship makes it more personal. The other thing that touches me so deeply about the story is the tender love and overwhelming grief that rugged farmer felt for a little child who never matured into manhood.

Somehow, in that farmer's sobs and tears, I see the grief of God as He weeps over many of His own children who should have grown into spiritually mature men and women by now, yet remain pitifully stunted babes. Oh, how He must mourn as He is forced to lay aside His thrilling plans for their lives. What sorrow He must feel as He considers the mighty exploits they could have accomplished in His name. And how God must sigh as He grieves for the intimacy and friendship He and those beloved children are missing because they hardly know Him.

Spiritually Stunted Church

What has caused such a terrible tragedy in the Church? What happened to bring it all about?

Over the past few decades, we experienced a remarkable outpouring of the Spirit of God. In the 1960's and 1970's particularly, God sovereignly moved on the baby-boomer generation and reaped a harvest of souls. Thousands of churches came into existence to accommodate these new believers; thousands more experienced dramatic changes.

Churches became less a Sunday meeting hall and more a dynamic hub for genuine body life. Wooden religious traditions gave way to spontaneous worship. The exercise of spiritual gifts, such as healing and prophecy, increased, and some circles witnessed a resurgence of prayer.

Like a father eagerly participating in the birth of a child, I witnessed the emergence of this new life into the Church. Barely able to contain my excitement, I watched as a new generation of believers was supernaturally birthed.

What a potent force this multitude of believers would be when they were fully mature: equipped for the works of service, steadfast in the faith, wholly reliant on God, filled with integrity, wise in the ways of God and men! What impact they would have in turning men and women from godlessness and perversion and bringing healing to a nation festering with the wounds of sin. How God would be moved by the effective prayers of a fervent, righteous generation crying out for Him to visit the earth in power and fulfill His purposes.

Like a doting father hovering over the crib of his sleeping infant, I couldn't keep from smiling, anticipating the day when these tender, vulnerable young converts would cast aside the immaturity that marks all children and become strong believers firmly established in the ways of God. I sighed with satisfaction, imagining what a pleasure it would be to watch them growing in the character, wisdom, and knowledge of God and into the full stature of Christ.

But maturity was not to become the hallmark of this move of God. As a whole, the Church did not rise to become the powerful instrument the Lord could use to transform the nations. Rather than maturing into adulthood, some believers have never progressed beyond infancy or toddlerhood in their relationship with God. Many have remained fixated in the selfishness of childhood or the awkwardness of adolescence.

The Church is now filled with believers who have begun in the faith—they can profess a saving knowledge of Christ—but who have ceased to grow. As a result, a spiritually stunted Church has been plagued by immorality, carnality, worldliness, imbalance, and lack of direction. Until the Church grows out of spiritual infancy, such problems can only continue.

I believe God has appointed this hour for the Church to take its rightful place. It's time to put our childish ways behind us, casting aside everything that would hinder our growth in God. The time has come to get down to the business of assuming the responsibilities of spiritual adulthood. Simply put, it's time to grow up.

Three Stages in the Life of the Believer

We are not saved to stagnate. Conversion is not a goal; it is a gateway. We are to progress from strength to strength, from glory to glory.

Three groups, which represent three stages in the life of the believer, are addressed in First John 2:12-14: (a) *children*, who represent salvation; (b) *young men*, who represent maturation; and (c) *fathers*, who represent consummation.

Children: Conversion

The Christian life is meant to be progressive. Conversion is the starting place, not the stopping place. It's wonderful to know our sins are forgiven. It's fantastic to discover that old things have passed away and all things have become new. Nothing surpasses the reality of God's presence dwelling within us and of our becoming partakers of His divine nature. No wonder the writer of Hebrews calls this "so great a salvation" (Heb. 2:3). Yet conversion is merely the beginning of the new life we are to experience in Christ.

A spiritual child, like a natural infant, has many deficiencies. He lacks strength, wisdom, insight, and purpose. His world largely revolves around his own needs and desires. Others must spend vast amounts of time catering to his well-being, for he demands almost constant attention and protection. His ability to give is limited; his demands are limitless.

A child's satisfaction, as Paul told the Corinthians, is derived from childish things. Tragically, today, as in Paul's day, the Church is overrun with spiritual children, most of them content to live as babes demanding constant pampering and attention, having little regard for the needs of others, let alone the purposes of God.

Most of us can recall the awkwardness of making the transition from childhood into adolescence in the human realm. Bodies changing. Minds expanding. Relationships becoming more complex. Responsibilities increasing. With so many personal changes taking place, those years can be some of the most difficult of our lives. But if we are ever to make the transition to the next stage in the *spiritual* realm, change—as difficult and uncomfortable as it may seem—will be a part of that process. If we do not wish to remain children, we must be willing to let go of the old and embrace the new.

Young Men: Maturation

Next, John addresses the young men: those who have left behind their childishness. No longer satisfied with "kids' stuff," they realize there's more. Not content to remain immature, they hunger for the Word of God. As the process of maturation continues, they become strong, committed, and steadfast.

Maturity is measured not by the absence of problems in our lives, but by how we handle them. Upon entering this second stage, believers become aware of the spiritual conflict in which they are engaged. Unlike young children, who are largely spared from conflicts, young men and women must now rise up and conquer. They cannot be swayed by conflicts and circumstances.

As a very wise woman once observed, "So many of God's people are like thermometers—constantly changing, depending on their environment. Others are like thermostats—constant and consistent, regardless of their circumstances." God is desirous that people rise above their circumstances and learn to live consistent, victorious lives in the strength that He alone supplies.

Fathers: Consummation

Having looked at children and young men, we now focus our attention upon the fathers. I've often wondered why John wrote so little about this particular category. He offers specific statements about children, such as, "Your sins are forgiven you" and "You have known the Father" (1 Jn. 2:12-13 NKJ). To the young men he says, "You have overcome the wicked one" and "You are strong, and the word of God abides in you" (verses 13-14). But to the fathers, John says only, "You have known Him who is from the beginning" (verses 13-14). How does this differ from children, who also "have known the Father"?

The child, because of his limited understanding, knows God simply as "Father." Having experienced His love, forgiveness, provision, and protection, the child is happy and content to be showered with the Father's attention. He thinks the Father exists solely to satisfy his personal needs.

What, then, does John mean when he says that the *fathers* "know Him"? I believe John is referring to a deep revelation and understanding of God. Just as a wife knows her husband in a greater capacity than their children know him, so the fathers know God with deeper intimacy and insight than do the spiritual children.

Have you ever noticed that John uses the phrase "from the beginning" more than any other biblical writer? He opens his first Epistle with: "What was from the beginning..." (1 Jn. 1:1). John introduces his Gospel with, "In the beginning was the

Word, and the Word was with God, and the Word was God" (Jn. 1:1). And John begins the Book of Revelation with, "Him who is and who was and who is to come" (Rev. 1:4). Perhaps the key to understanding what John is saying regarding fathers lies therein.

John sees God as both the Alpha and the Omega—the beginning and the end. It is impossible to see things from God's perspective unless we know what was in His mind and purpose "from the beginning." The fathers have experienced salvation and maturation. But they have also progressed to know and understand the mind of God regarding His purpose for their lives and for the Church, as it relates to His eternal plan. That is why I chose the word *consummation* to describe spiritual fathers.

Succinctly put, *consummation* means "completion" or "fulfillment." In other words, God sees the whole, not just the parts. Only as we begin to understand what was in the mind of God from the beginning will we be able to recognize many of the perils of immaturity and avoid the errors and shortcomings of the unbalanced teaching that has become so prevalent in the Church today.

Understanding what God had in mind from the beginning also helps us gain a clearer perspective on current issues and situations. Take, for example, an incident from the life of Christ. When the Pharisees asked Jesus what He thought about divorce, He did not spout the results of the latest opinion poll. Instead, He immediately began relating the issue to the purpose God originally had in mind. "From the beginning," He said, "it has not been this way" (Mt. 19:8). Jesus was spiritually mature. He understood the mind, ways, and purpose of His Father God.

In a day of situation ethics, decaying morals, and no absolutes, we have a desperate need for "fathers" in the Church;

spiritually mature men and women; people who understand the mind and purpose of God as it pertains to His eternal plan; people who are not caught up in the cross-currents of popular trends, but who cry out for reality in their relationship with God; people who, having found the Pearl of Great Price, are willing to give up all to own it.

Sandbox Christians or Spiritual Fathers?

But we do not become "spiritual fathers" overnight. Maturing takes time. Maturing requires adjusting to change.

We all struggle with change, no matter what our age, because it's usually more comfortable to hang back and enjoy what's familiar. It's easier for young children to stay home and play with their toys than to begin school and sit in a desk most of the day.

In her beautiful book, *In My Father's House*, the beloved Corrie ten Boom recalls how her first day of school was marked by tears and tantrums as she mourned the loss of familiar routines and protested her lost freedoms.

> "My doll, Casperina, and I were going to have a party! Mama and Tante Anna were cooking, and I watched their long skirts bustle past me from my perch on the footstool beneath the table. This was a wonderful place to play, safe and secure beneath the red and black tablecloth...
>
> "I clutched Casperina's three-fingered hand in mine and whispered, 'We'll just stay in our own secret place....' "

However, as Corrie recalls:

> "A time comes when all children, even a little Dutch girl with her jaw set and her black-stockinged legs rigid upon the staircase, must leave her father's house for a time....
>
> " 'I'm not going to school. I know how to read; I can learn arithmetic from Papa, and Casperina needs me at home.'

"There. *That* was settled.

" 'Of course you're not going to school alone, Corrie. I am going to walk with you.'

"Papa bent over me, his beard tickling the top of my head, and one by one loosened my fingers on the railing. With the release of each finger, I howled a bit louder. By the time Papa had my hand in his, he was almost dragging me down the street toward school. I thought my hand would break...and then it would be impossible for me to go to school.

"It must have taken a great dignity for Papa, with his immaculate suit and erect carriage, to struggle past the homes and shops of his friends with a red-faced child announcing her objections to the entire world.

"I knew my Father was not angry, but his will was law. I had to obey.

"When we arrived at the school, I saw a little boy being carried into Master Robyn's classroom in his father's arms. (At least I was walking!) He was crying lustily, even louder than I was. He looked so ugly that I felt sorry for him. But what about me? I realized how I must look to others, and stopped abruptly.

"Papa released my hand; my fingers weren't broken at all—only my heart was slightly injured. However, when Papa kissed me gently on the cheek...he assured me that when school was over, he would be waiting at home, and I knew I would find that blessed security I needed in the shelter of his arms...."[1]

You and I can identify with little Corrie because some of these same feelings surface when God enrolls us in His school of the Spirit. We tend to resist accepting new responsibilities and restrictions. "This is too hard," we grumble tearfully. "It requires too much." Some of us long to return to the familiar backyard and play in the sandbox.

But God's goal is not to raise a generation of sandbox Christians. It's fine for children to play and putter around in the sand, but grown-ups who insist upon remaining at that level of maturity will never enjoy the satisfaction of being used of God.

Their lives will be wasted on foolish, fruitless pleasures rather than fulfilling God's purpose in their generation. They will never experience the rich rewards promised to those who press forward to maturity in God.

A Time to Let Go

Tying an incident later in life to her experience as a child on her first day of school, Corrie tells how her heavenly Father was also forced to "loosen her fingers on the railing" to prevent her from missing the greater blessings and purposes He had planned for her life.

"I had been traveling so much and was tired—tired of strange beds and different food—tired of dressing for breakfast—tired of new people, and new experiences. I liked this very luxurious house with its large rooms, and decided to stay, and enjoy the comfortable life in Holland, although I knew that God didn't agree with my decision.

"Most of the furniture in the entire house was mine, but there was one room in particular which reminded me of the happy family life of my past. It was a room which held my treasures: photographs of those I loved, mementoes of my family during the years before. Every picture was like the railing on the stairs. My hands grasped the past, and tried to hold on, but my heavenly Father's hands were stronger....

"My heavenly Father spoke to me, 'Only obey Me, Corrie. I'll hold your hand. It is My will that you leave your room.

Later you will thank Me for this experience. You do not see it, but this is one of My great blessings for you.'

"Father's hand was firm, but I knew His love.

"I packed my suitcase again and left for the United States. How the Lord blessed my time there. Meetings began to grow in size, and when I saw people come from darkness to light, from bondage into liberation, I began to see the pattern. I could praise my Father that His hands were stronger than mine."[2]

The freedom and security of childhood can be wonderful. Cherished memories can be comforting. But the soul cannot be nourished for long on sweet memories. We cannot go on with God if we insist upon keeping one foot on the comfortable, secure ground of the past. We must be willing to release the past, place our hand in the strong hand of our heavenly Father, and allow Him to enroll us in the school of His Spirit if we are ever to reach maturity and experience the fulfillment of His wonderful purpose.

Are you still a spiritual child? Are you still cutting your spiritual teeth and toddling around when you should be teaching others to walk in the Spirit? Lay aside your toys. Reach up and take your Father's hand. The school bell is ringing. It's time to grow up.

Endnotes

1. Corrie ten Boom and Carole C. Carlson, *In My Father's House* (Old Tappan, New Jersey: Fleming H. Revell Co., 1976), pp. 36-37.

2. ten Boom & Carlson, *In My Father's House*, pp. 37-38.

Chapter Two

Understanding the Purpose of the Cross

For more than 14 years my family and I lived in New Zealand, home to some of the world's most spectacular scenery. While driving its windy roads, it was not unusual to pass a beautiful vintage automobile dating back 50 or 75 years.

Owners labored for untold hours and at great expense, restoring these cars to their original condition. Nothing was overlooked in the process. Every part had to be painstakingly checked, stripped, repaired, or replaced before being fitted back together.

The Importance of Authenticity

Imagine with me a man who stumbles across one of these cars in the back of a farmer's shed. For the sake of our story, let's say it's a 1913 Model T. Realizing the car's potential if restored, the man offers the farmer some cash and becomes the proud owner of what was once a beautiful car.

Eager to see the car restored, the man spends every spare minute working on it. The weeks turn into months, but every day he sees a little more improvement.

There's a problem, however. You see, this fellow has never seen a 1913 Model T in its original condition, so he has no idea what it should look like. His knowledge of cars is largely governed by today's standards and styles.

Determined to restore the car as quickly and inexpensively as possible, the new owner settles for readily available parts. Rather than checking out the manufacturer's specifications for the original wheel hubs and road wheels, he simply buys some mag wheels with wide tires. Rather than using the specified brass-plated headlights and lamps, he settles for some small square halogen ones. Instead of using a vintage-style dashboard and firewall crafted in wood veneer, he substitutes plastic and anything else he can make fit. Rather than upholstering the seats in genuine leather, he settles for a bright plaid fabric. And so it goes for every single thing he restores.

Eventually the wonderful day comes when the car is finished. The owner proudly drives around town displaying his achievement. As the fellow rides past a retirement complex, he notices an elderly man rise from a rocking chair on the front porch, staring in disbelief. Supposing that the old gentleman has been overcome by nostalgia, the owner wheels the car into the driveway and invites the man to look the car over and tell him what he thinks.

Imagine his shock and disappointment as the old man shuffles slowly around the car, scratches his head, and says, "I used to own one of these, young fellow, so I know what I'm talking about. This car looks nothing like the original model!"

Christians today are like that sincere, but naive, car buff. Unknowingly, we have settled for a cheap imitation of the real gospel. I'm convinced that if we were to meet a first-century believer, he or she would stare at us in disbelief. Although we proudly call ourselves "Christians," I'm afraid we're a far cry from the genuine Christianity described in the Owner's Manual—the Word of God.

The Need for Balance

"There is nothing so likely to lead to error or heresy as to start with the parts rather than the whole," said Dr. Martyn Lloyd Jones. Would that every believer understood the importance of that profound observation.

Never before has the Church been so bombarded with such an infinite variety of "parts." A visit to the local Christian bookstore will reveal an almost limitless variety of topics, each vying for your attention and money. The shelves are sagging under the weight of new books—everything from diets to depression and fitness to faith. No wonder the average believer has little sense of direction or purpose. Ignorant of the whole purpose of God, he stands bewildered among the "parts."

For many, the local church has become an alternative to the country club. Membership is easily gained through baptism and tithing. Few ever stop to ponder the reason for the Church's existence. Content to attend a bare minimum of meetings, these believers settle into apathy and boredom, indifferent to their true purpose and calling.

As if indifference and apathy are not enough to hinder most Christians on the road to maturity, strange winds of doctrine are also blowing all about us. Every year it seems a new seminar superstar arrives center stage with his guaranteed formula for spiritual success. Backed with slick advertising, glossy manuals, and dynamic personalities, these self-anointed "oracles of wisdom" convince many immature believers that they, at long last, have discovered the answer to all believers' spiritual problems.

The promised results of such programs are usually short-lived. God never intended the "part" to replace the "whole." If we're going to press on toward maturity, we desperately need to return to "rightly dividing the Word of God." Only the whole counsel of God produces whole Christians. Anything less results in spiritual deformity.

"Carburetor" Christianity

Suppose someone is giving a lecture series to a group of students totally unfamiliar with how an automobile engine works. But the instructor, rather than presenting an overall view, chooses to concentrate solely upon the importance of the carburetor.

First he draws a diagram showing how a carburetor operates and what function it performs. Then he spends hours explaining every detail of its makeup, from the air cleaner to the jets. Next, the instructor painstakingly describes the various types of carburetors—the one barrel, two barrel, and four barrel. Finally, he closes his lectures by emphasizing once again how vital the carburetor is—after all, without it, the engine cannot possibly run. The hearers, still unfamiliar with the other components of an engine, leave the classroom preaching "the gospel of the carburetor."

Meanwhile, across town, another group listens attentively to a series of lectures on the role of the spark plug. Great detail is given as to its essential function. Diagrams are shown explaining exactly how the spark plug works. This lecturer also closes with a strong emphasis on the vital role played by one particular part of the engine, stressing that without the spark plug, it is powerless and unable to run. Now we have a new group proclaiming "the gospel of the spark plug."

Later, another group forms, extolling the virtues of the distributor. Not only do they claim its absolute necessity, they also begin to preach against the carburetor and spark plug. According to them, the distributor is the one and only true "gospel."

Similar teaching in the body of Christ has caused believers to become unbalanced and unwise, lacking the whole counsel of God. Congregations and followings form around these various "parts," convinced they have the ultimate and complete truth and shunning all who refuse to join them.

Paul faced a similar situation with the Corinthians. Not only were their loyalties divided—some claiming allegiance to Paul, some to Apollos, others to Christ—but they also stressed their own particular function without regard to the other parts of the body. The eyes were proud of their insight; the hands, of their service; the feet, of their support.

How desperately we need a new understanding of God's eternal, omniscient perspective. The Church is being swamped with wave upon wave of popular, appealing doctrines. Few want to hear about tribulation, discipline, sacrifice, or suffering.

While the Church grows fat, lazy, and indifferent to its real role in the earth, every year new advances are seen in the enemy's strategy. Islam continues to forge ahead with its militant zeal for world dominion. Cults increase, preying upon those who, thirsting for enlightenment, are content to drink from polluted springs.

Understanding God's Original Purpose

If we are to correct our gross errors and deficiencies, the Church must gain an understanding of the mind of God from the beginning. What was God's intention for mankind? Why did He create us in the first place? Only as we begin to comprehend the answers to these questions can we grasp the full significance of the cross.

Paul, in his epistle to the Colossians, writes:

For by Him were all things created, that are in heaven, and that are in earth, visible and invisible, whether they be thrones, or dominions, or principalities, or powers: all things were created by Him, and for Him (Colossians 1:16 KJV).

Most of us have little trouble believing God created everything. But when it comes to understanding we were created "for Him," we tend to feel our sovereignty is being threatened. In the Book of Revelation, John sheds further light on this vital truth:

Thou art worthy, O Lord, to receive glory and honor and power: for Thou hast created all things, and for Thy pleasure they are and were created (Revelation 4:11 KJV).

These two verses offer valuable insight into God's purpose in creating man. We were made for Him. We were created for His pleasure and purpose.

Before we seek a deeper understanding of the cross, it will be necessary first of all to study man in his original state before the fall.

We read in Genesis, "Then the Lord God took the man and put him into the garden of Eden to cultivate it and keep it" (Gen. 2:15). Immediately we notice three areas included in God's intention for man:

1.   Man's *submission*: "The Lord God took the man…"

2.   Man's *location*: "put him into the garden…"

3.   Man's *vocation*: "to cultivate it and keep it."

Man, as God intended, was originally under submission to His divine authority. He was placed in the location of God's choice and given the vocation that God intended him to have in order to serve His purpose. Clearly then we see man created, not only by God, but for God. There is no thought here of man determining his own course of action. Only after the fall do we see man living in independence, having turned to pursue his own way. Isaiah capsulizes this when he states, "All of us like sheep have gone astray, each of us has turned to his own way…" (Is. 53:6).

With this background, we can proceed with our understanding of the cross as it relates to God's intention for man. Perhaps our greatest error stems from the fact that we have failed to grasp God's purpose for man from the beginning. Because we are now governed by self-interest, our understanding of the cross has been distorted—hence, the cross becomes God's answer to "my" need. Our immediate response to the cross is, "What can I get out of it?" "What has the death of Christ accomplished for me?"

Why Did Christ Die?

Over the years, as I've ministered in various foreign countries, I've repeatedly asked the question, "Why did Jesus die?" Yes, Christ died to atone for sin. But was that the only purpose?

Let me use an illustration to help deepen our understanding of why Christ died. Suppose, for example, my wife and I have lived without transportation for many years. Finally, we have saved enough money to buy our first car. After days of shopping around, I settle on an automobile I believe to be suitable for our needs. The car, while in reasonable mechanical order, is far from tidy. The years and miles have taken their toll. Happily, though, I drive it home and begin cleaning it up.

As I remove the seats, I find a thick layer of grime and an assortment of lost coins and toys. The outside proves to be even more of a challenge. The paint has faded. Dust, dirt, and tar have laid claim to the finish. But slowly the grime is washed away and a new coat of polish brings a welcome shine. Now at last the car begins to reveal something of her former glory.

Upon finishing the job, I walk into the house and proudly display to my wife my bucket of filthy water. "Look at all this dirt, honey!" I exclaim. "See what all our hard work has accomplished!"

Well, obviously, something is terribly wrong. Nobody in his right mind would give all he had simply for a bucket of dirty water. My intention in buying the car was not its grime, but the car itself. The reason I gave all that I had was because I needed the car. I purchased it as my own to serve my purpose.

Let's take my "car" illustration even further and assume I had bought the car years before when it was brand new, ordering it special from the factory with a custom paint job and unique set of accessories. This car had been created just for me. Then, somehow over the years, we had parted and the car had been abused and neglected. Now at last I have found my car. I buy it back, and go about the difficult task of cleaning and restoring.

Although the illustration is far from perfect, it conveys a popular misconception about the cross. To most of us, the death of Christ served only one purpose: to wash the filth of sin from our lives. Yet, I'm not convinced God is so interested in our sin. The Bible says, "As far as the east is from the west, so far has He removed our transgressions from us" (Ps. 103:12). God obviously is not in the business of collecting sins.

The Cross: For Man's Benefit and God's Benefit

What then was His objective in going to the cross? As we search the Scriptures along these lines, we discover a twofold objective—one for man's benefit, another for God's.

As I've studied the Scriptures through the years, I've made a point to mark the verses dealing with the cross. Paul, in his epistle to the Romans, reveals the full meaning of Christ's death when he writes:

For not one of us lives for himself, and not one dies for himself; for if we live, we live for the Lord, or if we die, we die for the Lord; therefore whether we live or die, we are the Lord's. For to this end Christ died and lived again, that He might be Lord both of the dead and of the living (Romans 14:7-9).

Paul stresses that Christ's death was not merely for sin, but to once again establish His lordship over our lives. In his writings to Titus, Paul further clarifies this:

Who gave Himself for us, that He might redeem us from every lawless deed and purify for Himself a people for His own possession, zealous for good deeds (Titus 2:14).

Notice the two aspects of Christ's death. Paul beautifully ties together both man's benefit and God's intention. Man receives forgiveness and cleansing; however, Paul goes on to show that God desires man for Himself as His own possession. It is man, then, that God has in mind, not just his sin.

Further proof of this is shown in the Book of Revelation, where John sets forth the objective of Christ's death:

*Worthy art Thou to take the book, and to break its seals;
for Thou was slain, and didst purchase for God with Thy
blood men from every tribe and tongue and people and
nation* (Revelation 5:9).

These and other Scriptures cast fresh light on the cross and
the divine intention of God from the beginning.

We desperately need a fresh emphasis on the lordship of
Christ. For too long we have ministered an "easy believeism"
message that places no demands whatsoever upon the believer,
other than a trip to the altar, a quick prayer, and the promise to
tithe. Apart from this, we encourage new converts to keep clean
and await the rapture.

The Old Cross and the New

A.W. Tozer, in his indomitable way, sums up the problem
when he speaks of "The old cross and the new."

"Unannounced and largely undetected, there has come in
modern times a new cross into popular evangelical circles. It
is like the old cross; but while likenesses are superficial, the
differences are fundamental.

"From this new cross has sprung a new philosophy of the
Christian life, and from that new philosophy has come a new
evangelical technique—a new type of meeting and a new kind
of preaching. This new evangelism employs the same language as the old, but its content and emphasis differ.

"The old cross would have no truck with the world. For
Adam's proud flesh, it meant the end of the journey and carried into effect the sentence imposed by the law of Sinai.

"The new cross, in contrast, is not opposed to our flesh. It
is a friendly pal, the source of oceans of good, clean fun and
innocent enjoyment. It lets Adam live without interference.
His life motivation is unchanged—he still lives for his own

pleasure. But now he takes delight in singing worship choruses and watching religious movies instead of singing bawdy songs and drinking hard liquor. The accent is still on enjoyment, though the fun is now on a high plane morally, if not intellectually.

"The new cross encourages a new and entirely different evangelistic approach. The evangelist does not demand a surrendering of the old life before the new life can be received. He preaches similarities rather than contrasts. He seeks to create more interest in the gospel by showing that Christianity makes no unpleasant demands. His brand of Christianity offers the same things the world does, only on a higher level. Whatever the sin-mad world happens to be clamoring after at the moment is cleverly shown to be the very thing the gospel offers—only the religious version is better.

"The new cross does not slay the sinner; it redirects him. It steers him into a cleaner and jollier way of living and saves his self-respect. To the self-assertive it says, 'Come and assert yourself for Christ.' To the egotist it says, 'Come and do your boasting in the Lord.' To the thrill-seeker it says, 'Come and enjoy the thrill of success through Christ.' "[1]

Having been guilty of tampering with the truth, we need to return to the "ancient landmarks" and repent of our failings. One of the clearest verses regarding the cross is given in Paul's letter to the Corinthians. I believe this is the most concise statement in all of the Bible regarding the death of Christ: "And He died for all, that they who live should no longer live for themselves, but for Him who died and rose again on their behalf" (2 Cor. 5:15).

Revolutionizing Our Reason for Being

Jesus' death was to revolutionize our whole purpose in life. It was to mark the end of selfish living and put a roadblock in front of all our plans and purposes. Old things were to pass away; a new ministry and purpose were to begin (see 2 Cor. 5:17-18).

And yet so many in the church still live for themselves. Certain habit patterns have ceased. No longer do they continue to practice their former sins, but the root of self has never died. Their plans remain unchanged; they live for themselves—the very purpose which Christ died to destroy.

I know all about living for one's own selfish plans and purposes. You see, as a young person, before becoming a Christian, I dreamed of becoming a graphic artist. Being reared in a Christian home and having a father who was well-known as a preacher, I grew up hearing the claims of Christ. Although I knew I was a sinner and longed for the assurance of salvation, I resisted the gentle promptings of the Spirit for many years. Finally, at the age of 18, I surrendered my life to Christ. For three years before this, there were times when I would literally shake under the Spirit's conviction, yet I refused to respond. Why? Somehow, the Holy Spirit had made me aware that God was after more than just my sin—He wanted me. Not being prepared to give up my life and plans, I resisted, until finally I gave myself unreservedly to Him.

A portion of Scripture that has become increasingly real to me over the years says, "...You are not your own...you have been bought with a price... " (1 Cor. 6:19-20). Notice again the purpose behind the cross—you, not simply your sins, have been bought. Paul testifies: "Who loved *me*, and delivered Himself up for *me*" (Gal. 2:20, emphasis mine).

God Desires Us

By now we can begin to see something of the purpose of the cross. Far more is at stake than just our sins. God desires mankind—those "created by Him and for Him." Herein lies the weakness of much of our modern preaching and teaching. No wonder the Church (which is His body) lacks the zeal of its first love. No wonder thousands pass daily into a Christless eternity while the Church slumbers, unconcerned.

How well Paul understood the words, "You are not your own." He was made aware of it the moment of his conversion, when he cried, "What shall I do, Lord?" The Lord answered, "Arise, and go into Damascus and there you will be told of all that I have appointed for you to do." (See Acts 9:6.)

The word *Lord* implies submission. The command, "Go into Damascus," designates location. The instructions, "And there you will be told of all that has been appointed for you to do," indicates vocation.

How we need to return to the biblical basis of conversion! The easy believeism of today has produced a weak, pathetic Church, constantly in need of spiritual "pep-me-up" to keep it going. The average believer lives as an enemy of the cross— refusing its demands, but expecting to enjoy its privileges. Paul makes reference to these when he writes:

For many walk, of whom I often told you, and now tell you even weeping, that they are enemies of the cross of Christ ... who set their minds on earthly things (Philippians 3:18-19).

They are absorbed in earthly matters and this world is the limit of their horizon.

Where are the men and women today who know the joy of full surrender, who are the people who grow up, past spiritual infancy, to be mature in Christ?

- Those prepared to "follow the Lamb whithersoever He goeth."

- Those prepared to "forsake all and follow Him."

- Those who genuinely "seek first the Kingdom of God."

- Those who can say with Paul, "The things that are seen are temporal, but the things which are not seen are eternal."

- Those whose response is, "I delight to do Thy will."

- Those "of whom the world was not worthy."

- Those who "count not their lives as dear to themselves."

- Those whose goal is to hear Him say, "Well done, thou good and faithful servant."

Only as we begin to study the Scriptures afresh, do we begin to see how much of the Church remains in spiritual infancy. I was alarmed some years ago to read Peter's warning:

But false prophets also arose among the people, just as there will also be false teachers among you, who will secretly introduce destructive heresies, even denying the Master who bought them, bringing swift destruction upon themselves (2 Peter 2:1).

Notice Peter's warning of a teaching that will gradually creep into the Church, the end result of which will deny Christ the lordship over those He has purchased—those whom He created for Himself. It would appear that this is simply another way of saying, "We will not have this man reign over us—crucify Him." We accepted His provision of forgiveness, but we deny Him the right to enlist us in His purpose.

In view of all this, how should we respond?

Maturity Requires Surrender

First, we need to present ourselves unreservedly to the Lord in total surrender. The cross represents death—death to our own desires, plans, ambitions, and goals. The cross is final and complete.

Second, now that we are dead to self, we need to live for Christ. In order to fulfill this, we need to ask, "Lord, what will You have me to do?"

James in his epistle warns:

Look here you people who say, Today or tomorrow we are going to such and such a city, stay there a year, and open up a profitable business. How do you know what is going to happen tomorrow? For the length of your lives is as uncertain as the morning fog—now you see it; soon it is gone. What you ought to say is, If the Lord wants us to, we shall live and do this or that. Otherwise, you will be bragging about your own plans, and such self-confidence never pleases God. Remember, too, that knowing what is right to do, and then not doing it, is sin (James 4:13-17 TAY).

It is only when we recognize that we were "created by Him and for Him" and then respond by giving ourselves back to Him, that we can find and fulfill the purpose for which we were created. Only then can we become authentic replicas of Him in whose image we were created.

Endnotes

1. A.W. Tozer, *The Best of A.W. Tozer* (Baker Book House Co., 1978). Used by permission of Christian Publications, Camp Hill, Pennsylvania.

Chapter Three

Serving God's Purpose in Your Generation

A single woman who has an absolutely brilliant mind, but who, because of feelings of inferiority and fear of failure, chooses jobs far below her capabilities rather than attending graduate school and pursuing a professional career, shared with an older friend a troubling dream she'd had. "I saw a hand sorting through alphabetized manila folders in a large file. The hand pulled out the folder that had my name on it, then right across the front was stamped one word in big, red letters: "WASTED."

Like that Christian woman, many believers do not feel that their lives are counting for a divine, definite purpose, although they can readily share a testimony of their conversion experience. These Christians know they are saved and will make it to Heaven, but they're wandering through their divinely allotted time on earth feeling frustrated and unfulfilled.

A sailor, when asked where he sailed, responded, "I'm restricted only by the ocean." Are you, like that sailor, void of any real sense of direction? Are you drifting through life aimlessly and without purpose?

"A saved soul, but a lost life...." That's how Alan Redpath described it. What a waste. What a senseless tragedy, for the Scriptures clearly state that "God has saved us and called us...according to His *purpose* (2 Tim. 1:9, emphasis mine).

No Sense of Vision

Why is there so much boredom, restlessness, and unfulfillment in the Church today? I believe the problem stems from the fact that many believers have no sense of vision, no understanding of God's divine purpose for their own lives or for His Church as a whole.

For many Christians, the Bible seems like a huge jigsaw puzzle with thousands of bewildering, seemingly unrelated, pieces of information. Practically every service, sermon, or seminar seems to deal with another piece of the puzzle. Never having caught a glimpse of the "whole"—the overall "big picture" of the Word of God—they simply lay the Scriptures aside or content themselves with dutifully performing their daily Bible-reading ritual, convinced that the message of the Word of God is simply too complicated to understand.

Little wonder, then, that such Christians have no sense of vision. Satisfied with salvation alone, they give little thought to understanding God's divine purpose, or to finding their own place in God's plan—the destiny for which they were created.

How often I've been challenged by this gripping summary of King David's life:

" *'I have found David, the son of Jesse, a man after My own heart, who will do all My will.'... For David, **after he had served the purpose of God in his own generation,*** *fell asleep, and was laid among his fathers...* " (Acts 13:22,36, emphasis mine).

Serving the purpose of God in our own generation. That is our high calling. That is where we find true fulfillment. Nothing surpasses it; nothing satisfies apart from it. To be joined together with Christ, laborers together, united in spirit, intent on one purpose. What a privilege! What a calling!

But what is the purpose of God? How can we possibly serve it if we do not even know what His purpose is? To discover God's purpose, we must go back to the beginning. Perhaps as we start to see the "whole," we will be brought to "wholeness" ourselves.

God's Promise to Abraham

Abraham was called into the purpose of God:

...Get out of your country, from your family and from your father's house, to a land that I will show you. I will make you a great nation; I will bless you and make your name great; and you shall be a blessing. I will bless those who bless you, and I will curse him who curses you; and in you all the families of the earth shall be blessed (Genesis 12:1-3 NKJ).

Abraham's blessing was not only to be *retained*, it was to be released. God's desire was that through Abraham, all the nations of the earth would be blessed.

Centuries later, when speaking of God's purpose for Abraham, Paul explained:

And the Scripture, foreseeing that God would justify the Gentiles by faith, preached the gospel beforehand to

Abraham, saying, "All the nations shall be blessed in you" (Galatians 3:8).

Even before Israel was formed as a nation, God was revealing His purpose. In Genesis 13:14-15, God spoke to Abraham again:

...Lift up now thine eyes, and look from the place where thou art northward, and southward, and eastward, and westward: For all the land which thou seest, to thee will I give it, and to thy seed for ever (KJV).

Romans 4:13 reveals the deeper meaning behind God's promise to Abraham: "For the promise that he would be the heir of the world was not to Abraham or to his seed through the law, but through the righteousness of faith" (NKJ). God had a far greater purpose for Abraham and his seed than merely owning a plot of ground in the Middle East. God's intention was that he would become "heir of the world." The whole human race was in the mind of God when He called Abraham.

God's Promise to Israel

Descending from the 12 sons of Israel (the name conferred by the Lord upon Jacob, Abraham's grandson), the nation of Israel was formed. Israel was to be another link in the chain of God's purpose upon the earth. The nation was to be His instrument of witness to the nations. G. Campbell Morgan summarizes very clearly God's intention for Israel:

"It is important that we should understand the meaning of the creation of this nation. It cannot be too often emphasized that it was not the election of a nation from among others in order that upon that nation God might lavish His love while He abandoned the others. The purpose of God was far wider than that of the creation of this nation. It was that of the creation

36

of a testimony through this nation, for the sake of the others. The divine intention was the creation of a people who under His government should reveal in the world the breadth and beauty and beneficence of that government; a people who gathered in their national life about His throne and His altar, obeying His commands and worshipping Him, should reveal to outside nations the meaning of the Kingdom of God. It was not the election of a pet, but the creation of a pattern."[1]

Have you ever been in a classroom where the teacher chose one special pupil to be a "pet," the object of the teacher's affection, love, and attention? If so, you know how such actions can make the other students begin to feel almost second-rate. Israel was meant to be God's pattern, not His pet.

A "pet" is one thing, but a "pattern" is something altogether different. For example, if you know much about dressmaking, you know that a seamstress can take a pattern, and from that one pattern make multiplied numbers of dresses.

Through Israel, God wanted to establish a pattern that the other nations could look on and desire to be like. As His people gathered around His throne and His altar, obeying His commands and worshiping Him, they would reveal to outside nations the true meaning of God. In other words, Israel's lifestyle was to reflect the nature and character of God, and her laws were to point to His goodness.

Remember God's promises to Israel as a nation in Deuteronomy 28? Israel, provided she walked in obedience to her God, would remain undefeated. Her crops would flourish. The people would be healthy, unafflicted by the diseases other nations had. As they taught their children the Word of God, the nation's family life would be in order, and there would be no rebellion.

As a result, the other countries, looking upon Israel, would not be able to keep from comparing Israel's God to their gods. "Every time we go out to battle," they'd say, "we get defeated. Our kids are rebellious and into all kinds of trouble. Crime, violence, divorce, abuse, and dysfunctional families have become the norm among us. Deadly diseases are rampant. Our economy is in jeopardy, and we live in constant fear of being wiped out by the army of some enemy nation. What is it about you people that is so different?"

Israel would reply, "Well, there's nothing about us, in one sense, that is different. But, you see, we have a good God, a God who provides for us and blesses us. Our God has given us wonderful laws and principles for living. As long as we obey Him and walk in His ways, we don't have the problems other nations have."

Then the other nations would say: "Is there any chance of your God becoming our God? Could we join you?"

That, very simply stated, was God's intention. Israel was to be a pattern and example for other nations, but she was not chosen because of any merits of her own. Israel was simply raised up by God to be an instrument of His purpose.

But Israel did not understand this. Instead, she became proud and exclusive. Blinded to her calling and proud of her position, Israel gladly received all God's blessings, but failed in her commission to serve God's purpose.

God repeatedly sought to correct Israel through His prophets, but she refused to respond. As the nation became increasingly callous to the privilege of being God's instrument, the Lord spoke to her through Isaiah, the prophet:

...It is a light thing that thou shouldest be My servant to raise up the tribes of Jacob, and to restore the preserved of Israel: I will also give thee for a light to the Gentiles, that thou mayest be My salvation unto the end of the earth (Isaiah 49:6 KJV).

Misunderstanding her purpose, Israel became a narrow-minded, strongly prejudiced sect. Refusing to have anything to do with the other nations, Israel kept her wonderful revelation of God all to herself.

Suppose I were teaching a class and wanted to use an example to demonstrate Israel's tragic failure as God's instrument. Let's imagine that I took an expensive pen out of my pocket and held it up for all to see, explaining that I wanted everyone in the room to touch the pen and briefly examine it.

Next, suppose I handed my pen to a young man in the front row with the instructions that he was to look it over and pass it on to the person beside him. As long as everyone obeyed my instructions, each student in the room would have personally handled my pen within just a few minutes.

But suppose the young man in the front row said, "Wow! That's a great pen! It's just what I've been needing!" and stuck it in his pocket, ignoring my instructions to pass it on. Basically, that's exactly what the nation of Israel did. God said, "Be a pattern. Pass My message on to other nations, and My purpose will be established." Instead, Israel pocketed the blessings of God for herself. As a result the purpose of God was frustrated.

God's Promise to the Church

When Israel failed in God's commission to be a light to the people all around her who lived in spiritual darkness, God sent His own Son "to confirm the promises made unto the fathers," Abraham, Isaac, and Jacob (Rom. 15:8b KJV).

What does it mean to "confirm" the promises? I've done a reasonable amount of traveling in my life, and I've noticed that when I book my ticket, at the bottom of the itinerary usually appears a statement similar to this one: "Please reconfirm your booking within 24 to 36 hours before departure." I might have purchased a ticket three months ahead of time, but prior to my departure I should call the airlines; give them my name, destination, and flight number; and revalidate or reconfirm the arrangements I made months before.

Jesus Christ came to revalidate and reconfirm the promises God established way back in the Old Testament with Abraham: His promise that through Abraham's seed all the nations of the earth would be blessed. Even though Israel failed miserably, the promise was fixed in God's heart, and He refused to let it drop.

Through Jesus Christ, God purposed to reach all the nations of the earth: "Now to Abraham and his Seed were the promises made. He does not say, 'And to seeds,' as of many, but as of one, 'And to your Seed,' who is Christ" (Gal. 3:16 NKJ).

Some Christians may breathe a sigh of relief after reading that verse. "Whew, I thought God was about to nail me with the responsibility of reaching the nations of the earth with the gospel. If the seed is Christ, I don't have to worry about it. I'm off the hook."

But along comes verse 29: "And if you are Christ's, then *you* are Abraham's seed, and heirs according to the promise" (Gal. 3:29 NKJ, emphasis mine). As Christians, you and I are Abraham's seed.

Because Israel failed to accomplish God's purpose in the earth, Jesus declared to the scoffing chief priests and Pharisees: "Therefore I say to you, the kingdom of God will be taken from you and given to a nation bearing the fruits of it'' (Mt. 21:43 NKJ).

Who is that nation? We find the answer in First Peter 2:9 (NKJ): "But you are a chosen generation, a royal priesthood, *a holy nation....*" Why? "...That you may proclaim the praises of Him who called you out of darkness into His marvelous light."

As the holy nation to which Christ referred, the Church has a divine mandate and responsibility to reach the nations of the earth with the gospel. You and I have the magnificent privilege of being used to help accomplish God's purpose in the earth.

Catching the Vision

If you read the *Reader's Digest*, you know that a condensed form of a best-selling book appears in the back of the magazine each month. While leaving the basic essence and message of the book intact, the editors reduce the book to a fraction of its original number of pages.

That's remarkable, but Jesus gave us the ultimate condensed book when He reduced the entire Old Testament to two verses: Luke 24:46-47! During Christ's appearance to His disciples after His resurrection, He said:

> ... *"These are the words which I spoke to you while I was still with you, that all things must be fulfilled which were written in the Law of Moses and the Prophets and the Psalms concerning Me." And He opened their understanding, that they might comprehend the Scriptures. Then He said to them, "Thus it is written, and thus it was necessary for the Christ to suffer and to rise from the dead the third day, and that repentance and remission of sins should be preached in His name to all nations, beginning at Jerusalem"* (Luke 24:44-47 NKJ).

41

Essentially, Jesus was saying, "If you want the basic ingredients of what Moses, all the prophets, and the psalmists were talking about, it's this: A Seed would come, die, and be resurrected, and repentance and forgiveness of sins in His name would be proclaimed to all nations." Then, in verse 48, Jesus adds, "And you are witnesses of these things."

We are witnesses of the gospel, not in the sense of "witnessing" a car accident taking place, but in the sense of being responsible for and proclaiming the message of the gospel.

But as important as that message is, Jesus told His disciples not to rush out immediately to spread the Good News. Instead, He commanded:

...Tarry in the city of Jerusalem until you are endued with power from on high (Luke 24:49 NKJ).

Now we are beginning to see more of the puzzle pieces coming together. Once we catch a glimpse of the overall picture of the gospel, we see the reason for the baptism of the Spirit: to anoint us for service and enable us to be witnesses. We see the reason for the gifts of the Spirit: to enable us to serve God powerfully, efficiently, and effectively as we edify the body of Christ and spread the gospel to others. We see the reason why the Scriptures contain so much instruction on holy living and family life: so our light may so shine before men that they will see our good works and glorify our Father in Heaven.

The Apostle Paul understood this, and his entire life and ministry were riveted upon fulfilling God's great purpose. When recounting his testimony to King Agrippa, Paul declared: "And now I stand and am judged for the hope of *the promise made by God to our fathers*" (Acts 26:6 NKJ, emphasis mine). Then Paul explained the exact focus of the calling he received from Christ:

So I said, "Who are You, Lord?" And He said, "I am Jesus, whom you are persecuting. But rise and stand on your feet; for I have appeared to you for this purpose, to make you a minister and a witness both of the things which you have seen and of the things which I will yet reveal to you. I will deliver you from the Jewish people, as well as from the Gentiles, to whom I now send you, to open their eyes in order to turn them from darkness to light, and from the power of Satan to God, that they may receive forgiveness of sins and an inheritance among those who are sanctified by faith in Me." Therefore, King Agrippa, I was not disobedient to the heavenly vision (Acts 26:15-19 NKJ).

Paul understood that Christ had appeared to him to anoint and appoint him to be a proclaimer, a priest, to the Gentiles. And notice his next words to Agrippa:

...I stand, witnessing both to small and great, saying no other things than those which the prophets and Moses said would come—that the Christ would suffer, that He would be the first to rise from the dead, and would proclaim light to the Jewish people and to the Gentiles (Acts 26:22-23 NKJ).

Paul had his motives and message straight. He understood what the whole purpose of the Church of the Lord Jesus Christ is about!

Israel misunderstood God's message and missed His purpose, but God is not yet through with this beloved nation. As Paul explained, "For if their being cast away is the reconciling of the world, what will their acceptance be but life from the dead? ... And so all Israel will be saved" (Rom. 11:15,26 NKJ).

Possessing the Gates

Please allow me to point out something very special, just in case you haven't noticed it before. In Genesis 22:17, God said to Abraham:

In blessing I will bless you, and in multiplying I will multiply your descendants as the stars of the heaven and as the sand which is on the seashore; ***and your descendants shall possess the gate of their enemies.***

Now compare Christ's words to Peter concerning the Church, Abraham's seed: "...Upon this rock I will build My church; and *the gates of hell* shall not prevail against it" (Mt. 16:18 KJV, emphasis mine). What hope that promise gives to us in a day when the enemy has been winning one victory after another against the people of God.

Richard J. Foster, in his penetrating book, *Prayer: Finding the Heart's True Home*, shares a personal experience that will speak to all who ache with longing to see and be a part of God's triumphant Church:

"In the spring of 1978 Carolynn and I drove to the Oregon coast for a few days of rest from a demanding winter schedule. On our first morning there I got up before the sun, though not before the sun's light. Carolynn was still asleep, so I quietly slipped out for an early walk on the beach. The tide was out, and the night mist was just beginning to flee.... Nearby was a huge monolith well known as Haystack Rock....With the ocean in retreat, I was able to walk almost completely around this magnificent rock fortress, which rises straight out of the sand. I marveled at its stubbornness in standing against the unrelenting attack of ocean waves....

"What happened next is hard to explain. I had come to a cliff overlooking the beach. On top was a forest of hemlock,

Sitka spruce, and Western cedar. I was admiring one giant Western cedar especially. I knew it took several centuries for this tree to attain its present size. Then, as I took three steps to the right, I saw what had been hidden from my view by the healthy tree—another extremely large but obviously rotting Western cedar. Some sprouts of green went out on two sides, but it would be only a matter of time before the tree died, for its center was exposed—apparently it had been struck by lightning in some far distant past. Aside from the huge size of the two trees, there was nothing unusual in the scene.

"But then, as I examined the decaying tree, the word of the Lord came to me, saying, 'This is My church!' When I heard the words, tears came to my eyes. I had worked in churches all my life, and I knew it was so—the Church, while huge and with some vestiges of life remaining, was decaying. Then, for some reason unknown to me, I turned 180 degrees and looked back at Haystack Rock in the distance. The tide had come in by now, and the rock was completely surrounded by water, the waves savagely breaking against it. The divine word continued, 'But this is what My Church is going to be.' "[2]

God's longing, God's heartbeat, is to reach the nations of the earth with the message of His eternal love and life through Christ. This is the ultimate reason for each little piece of the jigsaw puzzle in His Word. God's purpose will be fulfilled, and He is going to accomplish it through a mighty Church and through you and me individually—if we will allow Him to.

Wasters or Warriors?

Here lies an incredibly solemn warning: Just as God rejected Israel, having to bypass her in order that His purpose might be realized, God can set you, me, a congregation, or an entire denomination aside as well.

God can remove a church's candlestick. He can withdraw His anointing if you or I become proud, exclusive, and self-centered. He can withdraw His blessing if we try to keep the inheritance all to ourselves. And He can raise up other individuals, other congregations, other denominations, other nations who will do His bidding. God *will* build His Church; His eternal purpose *shall* be fulfilled.

We can squander our unique talents and giftings. We can miss our basic reason for being. But if we give ourselves totally to God for the fulfilling of His purpose—penetrating the darkness of this world with the light of His glorious gospel and building a Church triumphant—we will find meaning and fulfillment.

Now is the time to lay aside our childish, self-centered ways. Now is the time to embrace our holy calling and allow His power and light within to push back the darkness, possessing the gates of the enemy. Now is the time to rise up and serve the purpose of God in our generation.

Endnotes

1. G. Campbell Morgan, excerpt from *Living Messages of the Books of the Bible* (Westwood, NJ: Fleming H. Revell Company, 1912).

2. Richard J. Foster, *Prayer: Finding the Heart's True Home* (New York, NY: HarperCollins Pub., 1992), pp. 243-245.

Chapter Four

Hungering for Intimacy With God

Chiseled in stone over the beautiful entrance way to the Canterbury Museum in the city of Christchurch, New Zealand, appears this verse: "Lo, these are parts of His ways; but how little a portion is heard of Him?" (Job 26:14a KJV) How fittingly this describes the museum with its thousands of displays all attesting to God's marvelous handiwork, while giving little credit to God Himself.

Yet how poignantly that same verse describes the Church and, for that matter, the average believer. While we bask in all the blessings of God's provision, how little do we really hear of Him? Like spiritual babes, content with seeing His acts, we care little for knowing Him or His ways.

Growing in Intimacy With God

It's time to grow up. It's time for believers to come under the tutoring of God and become trained in His ways. Though many yearn to be part of God's purpose, they fail to understand that our involvement with God's purposes flows out of our intimacy with God.

Our personal relationship with God is the one basic prerequisite for an effective Christian life. Mark recalls that Jesus appointed 12, "…That they might be with Him, and that He might send them out to preach, and to have authority to cast out the demons" (Mk. 3:14-15). Like Gabriel, we need to stand in the presence of God before we are sent forth to proclaim His Word (see Lk. 1:19). To fail here is to fail everywhere. It is only as we come to know God and His ways that we can fully understand His mind and purpose.

There is far too much "spiritual" activity today that lacks the hand of God's blessing upon it. We have seen the television evangelists, who like the speech of Proverbs, constantly cry, "Give, give, give." The show goes on oblivious to the fact that God has long since removed His blessing. How desperately we need to return to a new hunger after His presence. Like the holy anointing oil of old, there can be no substitute. No wonder the Lord says:

Let not a wise man boast of his wisdom, and let not the mighty man boast of his might, let not a rich man boast of his riches; but let him who boasts boast of this, that he understands and knows Me, that I am the Lord… (Jeremiah 9:23-24).

Longing to Know God

The one common denominator of every effective saint of God has been a love for His presence. David, despite his failings, had a longing after his God. Time after time, he expressed in the Psalms his desire to know Him more intimately: "As the deer pants for the water brooks, so my soul pants for Thee, O God" (Ps. 42:1).

David, upon becoming king, wasted no time in seeking to return the ark, symbolizing God's presence, to its rightful place. Sadly, during the 40 years while Saul ruled, Israel had never sought after it. God save us from the same selfish, stubborn, sectarian state of seeking to operate independently of His presence.

We see David humbly acknowledging his need of God's presence, even after his failure to bring back the ark. He refuses to give up, but cries, "How can I bring the ark of God home to me?" (1 Chron. 13:12). Bound by his vow, he refuses to sleep, "...until I find a place for the Lord, a dwelling place for the Mighty One of Jacob" (Ps. 132:2-5). Oh, that men today were able in all honesty to say, "There is nothing on earth that I desire besides Thee."

Moses, likewise, valued God's presence above His promises. Following the idolatrous worship of the golden calf, God tells him to lead the people into the Promised Land. Not only is God prepared to keep His covenant promise, but He assures Moses that He will provide supernatural protection by sending His angel with him to drive out the various inhabitants of the land. One would have thought that Moses would rejoice. After all, this was the great longing of Israel—to have their own land and inheritance. God, however, after assuring Moses of His promise to keep His covenant, tells him that He won't go with them.

Moses now faces one of his most important decisions. He can proceed with leading the Israelites into their promised inheritance or remain in the wilderness. The choice would seem obvious—take the land. After all, wasn't this the whole reason for their deliverance from Egypt? The land was said to be flowing with milk and honey, typical of all the blessings God had provided for them: houses full of all good things that they would inherit, vineyards and olive groves that they never had to plant, cities that they didn't have to build.

God had provided all this for His people and, despite their sin, tells Moses He will keep His covenant and give it to them. Moses, however, refuses to settle for anything less than God's presence. He would rather stay with God's presence in the wilderness with its scorching sand and barren wastes than enter Canaan with all its "prosperity." God's presence was more important to Moses than anything else. Unlike many believers, pastors, and religious institutions today, Moses wasn't content with second best, even though it had the appearance of success.

Seeking God's Blessing Rather Than God Himself

Many today have tapped into God's covenant promises. They boast about their "homes and vineyards." Some even relate experiences where supernatural beings appeared before them or spoke to them. But strangely, their lives seem void of His presence. They've become satisfied with having God's blessing and provision and care little for His presence. Somehow they have lost sight of His "person" in exchange for what He can "produce."

Having bound God to His covenant promises, these believers have forced Him to honor His Word. But what of their relationship with Him?

Several years ago, my wife and I decided to move to another house. We advertised ours and were fortunate to find a cash buyer. The contract was signed and the date set for possession. Meanwhile, we had located another house only a few doors away from the first. After agreeing on a price and signing the necessary papers, we set the possession date of the other house to correspond with the vacating of our own. Everything went smoothly; we were amazed. Within 24 hours we had successfully sold one home and purchased another. Now all we had to do was wait.

Several days after, we were informed that the family who had purchased our house wanted to break their agreement. Our lawyer assured us that we didn't have to worry, the agreement could not be broken, for there were no conditions attached. They had given their word and signed an agreement indicating that they had the cash. Therefore, the law was in our favor. They had to keep their promise.

As my wife and I discussed the situation, we both came to the conclusion that, even though we had a contract (covenant), we would not enforce it. Having a right relationship with our would-be neighbor was more important to us than the "covenant."

Moses, not satisfied with second best, cries out to God: "If Thy presence does not go with us, do not lead us up from here." Then, explaining a primary reason why God's presence is so vital to him, Moses makes one of the most heart-searching statements found anywhere in the Word of God: "...so that we, I and Thy people, may be distinguished from all the other people who are upon the face of the earth" (Ex. 33:15-16).

The Hallmark of God's People

It's not our doctrine or creed, our laws or lifestyle that make us different. The one and only thing that makes you and me distinct is His presence. A singleness of desire after God is the hallmark of the true child of God. Paul was prepared to strip himself of all things in order to know Christ. David emphasized: "One thing have I desired of the Lord...to behold the beauty of the

51

Lord, and to inquire in His temple" (Ps. 27:4 KJV). What is your one desire?

In the Song of Solomon, we are given a glimpse into the relationship between a bridegroom and bride. We can learn many valuable lessons as we compare this couple's relationship with our relationship to the heavenly Bridegroom.

In the fifth chapter of this beautiful story, we are told by the bride how she is almost asleep when her beloved comes knocking on her door. Satisfied with her present condition, she hesitates, not wanting to arise and open the door. She has just taken off her clothes and bathed. She can't be bothered about arising and putting on her dress. Her feet are clean, and she's concerned about dirtying them again. As she pauses, counting the cost, her beloved continues to knock and express his love for her.

After some time, she arises and opens the door only to find her beloved has been grieved and has gone. Realizing her mistake, she starts searching for him. The cost now becomes greater than at first. She wanders throughout the city, inquiring if anyone has seen him. Struck and wounded, her shawl taken from her, she staggers on throughout the night searching and calling, but to no avail (see Song 5:2-6).

How often, I believe, the Lord comes to us, desirous of deepening His relationship, longing to spend time with us, yet we are content to repose, satisfied with having been washed and cleansed. We make little effort to arise and go deeper. But some believers, realizing they have missed out, arise and begin searching afresh. Undaunted by their circumstances, they refuse to give up until they find Him again.

As the story continues, the bride meets some of the daughters of Jerusalem. Longing for news of her beloved, she asks whether they have seen him. Unashamedly, she tells them how lovesick she is, and pleads that should they find him, they let her know.

The intensity of her longing makes quite an impression upon her listeners. Moved by her words, they long to know what sort of a person her beloved is. Suddenly she begins to pour out her love for him, describing in detail how wonderful he is. The bride explains that no one can compare with him. He's outstanding among thousands. Everything about him is desirable. She compares him to sapphires, ivory, alabaster, and gold. As her love for him unfolds, the women are anxious to meet him. Never have they heard of one so wonderful.

Our Desire Stirs Desire in Others

Only out of a deep, personal intimacy with our Beloved can we cause others to long after Him. Nothing else will satisfy. Nothing else is meant to satisfy. "This is eternal life, that they may know Thee, the only true God, and Jesus Christ whom Thou hast sent" (Jn. 17:3).

Like the church of Laodicea, we have become blinded to our true spiritual condition. Satisfied with our so-called prosperity and wealth, we continue on, oblivious to the fact that our "Beloved" is no longer in our midst. May God grant us the honesty to acknowledge our true condition and, like Moses, refuse to take another step unless we are certain of His presence going with us. An understanding of God's purposes is important; an understanding of His person is imperative!

Chapter Five

Learning to Fear God

Over the past 30 years or so, the Church witnessed an unprecedented move of the Spirit. Hundreds of thousands experienced new birth in Christ. Still others experienced the Charismatic renewal, and parched, withered spirits came alive to the things of God.

All over the world, believers fled their "old wineskins" in search of "new wine." Thousands of new churches sprang up, set apart from traditional churches by their joyous, spontaneous praise and worship. Eventually, the Charismatic movement gained worldwide attention. No longer could it be viewed as a small, isolated movement, for almost every major denomination had felt its impact.

Blessings and Problems

But many Charismatic Christians, seeking freedom from the bondage of denominationalism, eventually found themselves submitting to manipulative, self-serving demigods who refused to be accountable to anyone. Others, lacking sound teaching, fell prey to all sorts of strange doctrines and beliefs.

Liberty, for some, became license. Worship was weakened by cheerleading and hype. Praise gave way to pageantry and showmanship. Entertainment elbowed its way to center stage, and anointed ministry took a back seat.

Today the Charismatic movement has come and gone, and in the aftermath people are wondering what is happening. Instead of improving, the Church appears to be drifting farther and farther away from where it should be headed.

Stories of prominent Christian leaders' financial or moral failings have become headline news. Scores of lesser-known leaders have either resigned or have been forced to step down, leaving a trail of hurting and bewildered followers.

Believers are asking, "Who can we trust?" Some wonder if they'll ever believe in a leader again. And while some Charismatics are retreating to the mainline denominations they originally came out of, others are simply giving up. "I've had enough," they say in disgust. "You won't catch me in church again."

Perplexing questions abound. "What about all the prophecies and promises concerning revival? Problems seem to be worse now than they were 20 years ago. Where is the Church headed?" Christians everywhere seem confused by what's happening—and by what isn't happening.

Despite the extremes, multitudes have been blessed, transformed, and strengthened. Great has been the celebration! But now the Church is entering a new era.

Parallels for the Church Today

What should we make of all this? What is happening? Where are we headed? Can we find a corresponding set of circumstances in the Word of God to shed light on the frustrations and perplexities the Church is experiencing today? Interestingly enough, it is possible to draw several insightful parallels from a period in Israel's history described in First Chronicles 13–16.

Previous to that period of time, the ark of the covenant, symbolizing God's presence and forgiving love, had been the meeting place of God and His people, through their spiritual leaders.

The ark, a gold-covered, box-like structure measuring about four feet long, two feet wide, and two feet high, furnished the innermost shrine—the holy of holies—in the wilderness tabernacle of the Israelites. Hovering over the ark inside the holy of holies was the shimmering cloud of Shekinah glory, the visible presence of God.

As we are about to see, the history of the ark was in accordance with its intensely moral character. As a symbol of the Lord's presence, it was borne by the priests in advance of the host of Israel as they journeyed from place to place in their wilderness wanderings (see Deut. 1:33; Ps. 132:8). What a sight it must have been as the ark went before them, searching out a resting place for them to pitch their tents and showing the way they should go, with the cloud of the Lord billowing above them by day and a pillar of fire by night (see Num. 10:33; Deut. 1:33). At the ark's presence, the waters of Jordan separated before Israel, and as it was carried about Jericho, the walls fell (see Josh. 3:11-17; 6:4-20).

The tabernacle itself had to be dismantled and transported as the Israelites journeyed from place to place during their wilderness wanderings. The first site of the tabernacle in Canaan was probably in Gilgal (see Josh. 4:19). During the lifetime of Joshua, the tabernacle was settled in Shiloh.

Shiloh remained Israel's central sanctuary until the ark, which had been presumptuously carried into the battle of Ebenezer by the Israelites as their "good luck" piece, was captured by the victorious Philistines. It was also in this battle that

Hophni and Phinehas, wicked sons of Eli, Israel's high priest and judge, were slain after disgracing their priestly office in taking more than their share of the sacrifices and in their immoral actions in the tabernacle (see 1 Sam. 2:13-17; 4:17-18).

The terrified Philistines, after being ravaged by the destroying plague of tumors for seven months, sent the holy ark back to Israel in a cart (see 1 Sam. 5–6). The cow-drawn cart arrived in Beth-shemesh, a priest's city in Judah near the Philistine border, where the ark was received by surprised, but elated, Levites and a sacrifice was made to the Lord. However, when 70 or more men of Beth-shemesh were struck dead for their irreverence in daring to look into the ark, it was sent on to Kirjath Jearim to the house of Abinadab, where it remained 20 years (see 1 Sam. 6–7:1).

Later, the tabernacle was established at Nob, close to Saul's home in Gibeah. But after Saul massacred the priests for aiding David (see 1 Sam. 22:11-19), the tabernacle was transferred to Gibeon (see 1 Chron. 16:39; 21:29).

Saul, following his humble beginnings as Israel's first king, quickly became self-sufficient. During the 40 years of Saul's reign, we have no record that even once was inquiry made about the ark of God. Choosing to rely upon his own foolish, impulsive judgment, Saul rejected the commands of God.

When Saul refused to take correction, God had no choice but to raise up another king. Though outwardly Saul was still in control, God sent Samuel to anoint David king during Saul's reign. As David grew in favor, so did his following. "And everyone who was in distress, everyone who was in debt, and everyone who was discontented gathered to him" (1 Sam. 22:2a NKJ). Eventually, David replaced Saul as the one to whom the nation looked for leadership.

Aching for the Presence of God

The pattern I just described has been evident in many churches as well. The Saul type of leadership has left within many people a longing for reality. Not content to listen to "Saul talk," no matter how scholarly, they have ached for God's presence. In distress over the ways of men, discontented with the system, and in debt to God, believers have sought out leadership and churches where they could find a deeper relationship with the Lord.

Like so many believers today, David longed for God's presence. He had served under Saul's leadership. He had seen its deplorable weaknesses. David, determined to be a man after God's own heart, resolved not to enter his house or give sleep to his eyes until he found a dwelling place for God's presence (see Ps. 132:4-5).

I'm sure you know the story well, but I'll briefly recount it for you. Once David became king, he immediately set out to restore the ark to its rightful place, after being isolated for years in the house of Abinadab and cut off from Israel's worship. After consulting with his captains and leaders, David said to all the congregation: "...Let us bring again the ark of our God to us; for we did not seek it during the days of Saul" (1 Chron. 13:3 AMP). Finding everyone in full agreement with his purpose, David enthusiastically launched his plan to bring back the ark.

David and all Israel went to Kirjath Jearim. Reaching the house of Abinadab, they placed the ark on a "new cart," then proceeded toward Jerusalem, with David and the people merrily celebrating and making music before God with all their might.

Carried away with enthusiasm, David had not bothered to seek God for the right way to bring back the ark. Had he done so, he would have learned that during Israel's wilderness journeying, God had commanded that the tabernacle be carried on carts whenever it was to be dismantled and moved (see Num. 7:3-9). But the holy objects, such as the ark, were to be borne by the priests on their shoulders (see Num. 7:9).

You see, an elaborately worked veil separated the most holy place from the outer compartment of the tabernacle, and when the Israelites journeyed from place to place, the sacred ark was secluded from view by being wrapped in this curtain by the high priest and his sons. Then the poles of the ark were put into place so the priests could carry it upon their shoulders (see Num. 4:5-6). Consequently, the ark was normally seen only by the high priest, and that on very special ceremonial occasions.

God had expressly commanded that the ark was to be moved only by Levites. Furthermore, God had strictly forbidden even the Levites to touch the ark, lest they die (see Num. 4:15).

The heathen Philistines, in their complete ignorance of the ways and commands of Israel's God, had sent the ark back to Israel on a cart, and God had allowed it. But David was not an ignorant heathen. Had he and Israel's spiritual leaders taken time to study the law and inquire of God, seeking the Lord's explicit requirements instead of acting presumptuously, they would have known better.

A Place of Shaking

All went well for a time. In His mercy, God actually permitted the ark to be carried by a cart. The people, overcome with joy, celebrated before the Lord with their musical instruments. What a contrast to Saul's way of doing things. This was the real thing! God was in their midst! For most of them, this was a totally new experience.

How long the euphoric celebration lasted we don't know, but as they came to the threshing floor of Chidon, everything began to go wrong. The cart suddenly shook and lurched as the oxen drawing the cart stumbled. Uzzah, who was driving the cart, put out his hand to steady the ark, lest it topple. The anger of God was kindled against Uzzah when he touched the ark, and He smote him. In an instant, Uzzah lay dead.

The music and celebrating suddenly ceased. The panic-stricken crowd backed away. Only low murmurs penetrated the shocked silence. "Did anybody see what happened? Look! Uzzah is all slumped over. He must be unconscious. No...he's dead!"

Why was the judgment of God so severe? Everything had seemed to be proceeding so well...until the celebrating crowd came to the threshing floor. That's where the shaking began.

Losing the Fear of God

Why had the oxen stumbled when they came to the threshing floor? After all, a threshing floor is a level place, and God was quite capable of keeping the oxen steady.

There is a tremendous lesson for us here. The threshing floor was a place of separation, a place where the grain was separated from the chaff. Surely this was no coincidence. No, God hadn't had a temper tantrum. He had known exactly what He was doing.

David, who was just being launched into his career as king of Israel, had to be taught a very valuable lesson. It was not enough that David's motives were beyond question. His methods were clearly wrong, and God was not about to allow things to continue until lessons were learned and the necessary changes made.

Anger was David's immediate reaction. *Here I was, God, doing my best to honor and praise You, and You struck a man dead just because he touched the ark! Is this the result of my desire for You? Is this the kind of thing that happens when people seek Your presence?* No doubt such thoughts raced through David's mind as he pondered what had happened.

But that first rush of anger was immediately crowded out by fear. The Scriptures clearly state: "And David was afraid of God that day; and he said, How can I bring the ark of God home to me?" (1 Chron. 13:12 AMP) David was offended, and he was afraid. Yet, thank God, his desperate longing for the presence of the Lord had not ceased.

What was happening here? God was adjusting David. A maturing process was taking place. David was beginning to see God in a new light, and a holy, more reverent fear of the Lord was coming upon him.

God was telling David, "I'm not going to allow you and My people to continue as you have in the past. I am requiring a new respect, a new awe for My presence and for My ways."

But what about Uzzah? Like me, you've probably felt a lot of pity for him. Why was he punished so severely? Who was the poor guy, anyway?

The answer to that last question is a real eye-opener. We find the missing puzzle pieces in First Samuel 7:1-2 and Second Samuel 6:3-4. Remember Abinadab, the man in whose home the ark of God was cared for after the Philistines returned it? Uzzah was one of Abinadab's sons. Uzzah had grown up in the house where the ark had rested for 20 years.

Had the ark become commonplace to Uzzah? Had he become overly familiar with the things of God? Had he simply taken the presence and power of God for granted?

The prophet Samuel's account of the story makes it clear that this was the case. Samuel tells us that Uzzah died for his "irreverence" (see 2 Sam. 6:7).

Why are we seeing spiritual leaders falling right and left? Why are some towering Christian institutions beginning to crumble? I am convinced that the Church is approaching the threshing floor, and God is allowing some major shaking. Things simply cannot go on the way they've been. God is beginning to expose and separate the chaff from the grain. The Lord is being forced to get our attention because we have lost our fear of Him and our reverence and respect for His ways.

Like David and the people of Israel, we've had it all wrong. God is not seeking celebration. He is looking for sanctification. Praise without righteousness is not acceptable to the Lord.

Getting Back to Holiness

After Uzzah had been smitten by God, the proceedings ground to a halt. The ark was taken aside to the house of Obed-Edom, a Levite, where it stayed three months and during which time Obed-Edom was greatly prospered (see 1 Chron. 13:14).

In the meantime, David did some deep soul-searching. David prepared a place for the ark of God and pitched a tent for it in his capital city of Jerusalem (see 1 Chron. 15:1; 2 Sam. 6:12), but he left Israel's old tabernacle at Gibeon, where it stayed till the days of Solomon. It, together with the brazen altar, remained the place where sacrifices were offered (see 1 Chron. 16:39; 2 Chron. 1:3).

Let's stop a moment and consider this: What would have happened if David had been successful in bringing up the ark the first time? There had been nothing prepared for its return, yet preparation is essential to a return of the presence of God.

Do you recall the purpose of John the Baptist, the forerunner of Jesus? He was to go before Jesus in the spirit and power of Elijah, "…'to turn the hearts of the fathers to the children,' and the disobedient to the wisdom of the just, to make ready a people prepared for the Lord" (Lk. 1:17 NKJ). Preparing a people for the Lord was John's recurring theme:

> *The voice of one crying in the wilderness: "Prepare the way of the Lord; make His paths straight. Every valley shall be filled and every mountain and hill brought low; the crooked places shall be made straight and the rough ways smooth; and all flesh shall see the salvation of God"* (Luke 3:4b-6 NKJ).

We say we desperately desire God's presence. But we must prepare the way of the Lord, lest stumbling and smiting occur.

There's nothing wrong with scripturally based counseling, deliverance, and inner healing. There's nothing wrong with balanced teaching on faith, either. But the Church has become preoccupied with these things. What has happened to repentance? Whatever has happened to holiness and sanctification? Faith is wonderful, but what has happened to obedience? According to the Word of God, the supreme test of faith in God is obedience (see 1 Sam. 28:18).

David learned these lessons. Before he launched his second effort to bring back the ark of God, David prepared a place for it, he repented for his wrongdoing, and he determined to carry out and obey God's commands, not his own good ideas. "No one," he declared, "may carry the ark of God but the Levites, for the Lord has chosen them to carry the ark of God and to minister before Him forever" (1 Chron. 15:2 NKJ).

Sanctifying the Leaders

David now understood the need to have sanctified leaders who were prepared to carry the ark according to the Lord's instructions:

> *And David called for Zadok and Abiathar the priests, and for the Levites…. He said to them, "…Sanctify yourselves,*

you and your brethren, that you may bring up the ark of
the Lord God of Israel to the place I have prepared for it"
(1 Chronicles 15:11-12 NKJ).

These leaders had to cleanse themselves before they could
carry the presence of God. Isaiah warns, "...Be clean, you who
bear the vessels of the Lord" (Is. 52:11 NKJ).

Like David, the Church today must learn that God anoints
men, not methods. His presence rests upon people, not programs. Like David, the Church must learn to seek God for His
will, His timing, and His way. "For because you did not do it the
first time," David explained to the priests and Levites, "the Lord
our God broke out against us, because we did not consult Him
about the proper order" (1 Chron. 15:13 NKJ).

How readily you and I fall prey to the same mistakes. The
good becomes the enemy of the best. The still, small voice of
God is eclipsed by our own reasoning. Supposing there is only
one key that fits the problem locking up a certain situation, we
blindly follow the "successes" of others in that area.

Have you ever been involved in a church that had more "activity traps" than anointing? More programs than power? A
church where the pastor got most of his sermons from the seminars, books, and tapes of someone else? A church where the
people were kept so busy "feeding and tending the machine"
that they had no time to do the real work of the ministry?

How desperately we need to hear from God for ourselves.
How we need to simply bow and bask in His presence. So many
of us are carrying burdens God never intended for us to carry.
Somehow we've been deceived into thinking that the more we
do, the greater will be the outcome. But the results of that kind of
thinking can be disastrous: marriage and family breakdowns,

physical exhaustion, stress-related problems due to an unrelenting schedule of church and business meetings, etc. When the program demands all of a leader's time, everyone eventually pays.

Finding the Key

Hearing from God is the only key to real success. Remember how the prophet Amos warned of coming famine? A famine not of bread or water, but of hearing the voice of God (see Amos 8:11)? Notice that it was not a famine of God's *voice*, but of *hearing* His voice.

How do we hear His voice? By spending time alone in His presence. For some of us, this will come only by calling a halt to some of our schedules and programs until we hear God's voice and discern His will. As Solomon observed, "If the axe is dull and he does not sharpen its edge, then he must exert more strength…" (Eccles. 10:10). The more we delay sharpening the edge, the more strength, time, and energy will be required. The only way to sharpen an axe is to stop using it until once again its keen edge has been restored.

What a difference God's presence makes. Jesus said, "…Learn from Me…and you will find rest for your souls. For My yoke is easy and My burden is light" (Mt. 11:29-30 NKJ). The very mountains melt like wax at His presence (see Ps. 97:5). Most of our greatest obstacles would "melt" if we only sought God for His mind concerning them instead of relying upon our own resources.

Laying the Right Foundation

At threshing floors, David learned some of his greatest lessons about the folly and futility of presumption and self-reliance. The incident with Uzzah at Nachon's threshing floor was the first (see 2 Sam. 6:6-7). The incident with the Angel of the Lord at the threshing floor of Ornan was the second (see 1 Chron. 21:15).

You will recall how, after David numbered Israel, God was displeased with the king's reliance on human resources. As a result, He sent a pestilence upon Israel and destroyed 70,000 men. The Angel of the Lord was also about to destroy Jerusalem, but David was instructed by Gad, David's seer, to build an altar at the threshing floor of Ornan beside which the Angel of the Lord was standing. As David offered burnt offerings and peace offerings, and called upon the Lord, God answered him by fire from Heaven upon the altar. Then the Lord commanded the avenging angel to withhold any further judgment.

Then David said, "Here shall be the house of the Lord God and here the altar of the burnt offering for Israel" (1 Chron 22:1 AMP). The site of the threshing floor, which David purchased from Ornan, was to become the very foundation upon which Solomon was later to build the temple (see 2 Chron. 3:1).

It's vital that we grasp this principle. The foundation of the temple was a threshing floor, a place of separation. *Ekklesia*, from which we get our word "church," means "a calling out from."

Why is it, then, that the message of separation is so unpopular today? We hear a lot about health, wealth, and happiness, but holiness and sanctification—separation to God and setting apart from evil—are no longer in vogue.

Like David and the leaders and people of his day, how desperately we need to return to that holy fear which leads to a sense of awe and reverence in the presence of the Lord and a hatred for evil.

Therefore Come out from among them and be separate, says the Lord. Do not touch what is unclean, and I will receive you. I will be a Father to you, and you shall be My sons and daughters, says the Lord Almighty" (2 Corinthians 6:17-18 NKJ).

Surely that is the message for this hour.

Learning From Uzzah's Error

So, what is happening to the Church in the aftermath of the Charismatic movement? I believe God is shaking the Church, especially its leaders, to get our attention. In our childish ways, we have not taken seriously God's call to lead holy, sanctified lives. But spirituality cannot be separated from morality. We have a jealous God who seeks His rightful place in every area of our lives.

Uzzah's error should bespeak to all who long to grow up, to attain mature spiritual adulthood. Because of our casual irreverence and failure to seek the Lord's face, acknowledging Him in all our ways, God's judgment is falling on His house. Yet, even in the midst of judgment, God is gracious to His people. He is extending His hand in mercy, calling on us to repent of our irreverence and to separate ourselves unto Him in purity.

Make no mistake about it: The stern warning of John the Baptist to those seeking the presence of God in his day applies directly to us as well, for we, too, are approaching His threshing floor.

His winnowing fan is in His hand, and He will thoroughly clean out His threshing floor, and gather the wheat into His barn; but the chaff He will burn with unquenchable fire (Luke 3:17 NKJ).

There is no time to lose. You and I individually, and God's Church, collectively, must fall on our faces before God and cry out to Him in repentance. We must prepare the way of the Lord!

Chapter Six

Preparing the Way of the Lord

Drivers used to complain about how tough the Alaskan Highway was on cars. If only they'd known how tough it was on the men who made it!

The year 1992 marked the fiftieth anniversary of the 1,442-mile highway's existence. Although serious talk about such a road first surfaced in 1865, it took a bone-jarring motorcycle trip and the bombing of Pearl Harbor before talk turned into action.

When Louis Johnson, President Franklin Roosevelt's Assistant Secretary of War, commented that the Alaskan terrain he'd seen from the air was so rugged a man couldn't even lead a horse over it, C.C. Williams, an Alaskan prospector and dog musher, bet Johnson that a motorcycle could be driven over the route.

In May of 1939, Williams and a 25-year-old companion named John Logan, departed Fairbanks for Seattle, a distance of 2,300 miles, on motorcycles. Williams ultimately won his wager with Johnson, but the 201-day trip turned out to be a nightmare.

The first 90 miles were okay, but it took a couple of months just to cover the next 150. The men wound up pushing their motorcycles much of the way. Masses of fallen trees and impenetrable brush blocked the way, and the bike wheels frequently became mired in muskeg bogs so treacherous a man could sink out of sight if he stepped in the wrong place.

Dozens of racing streams and rivers also had to be crossed. Sometimes it was necessary to build rafts, put the machines on board, and paddle desperately.

Six and a half months after they started out, the emaciated bikers rumbled into Seattle, declaring that their journey proved a highway to Alaska was feasible.

The issue was settled once and for all two years later when the Japanese bombed Pearl Harbor. Fearing that a blockade of Alaskan seaports and an all-out invasion might be imminent, Roosevelt and his advisors decided that the highway, however difficult and expensive to build, must become a top priority.

In March of 1942, survey crews, guided by local trappers, started flagging a route, and by June, some 10,000 American troops had begun to advance a ragged track across the rugged terrain. Not long after construction began, 11 soldiers drowned when a makeshift raft sank. But despite this tragedy—and others that followed—construction continued at a frantic pace.

A famous advertisement recruiting civilian workers cautioned that employment would be:

"NO PICNIC. Men hired for this job will be required to work and live under the most extreme conditions imaginable. Temperatures will range from 90 degrees above zero to 70 degrees below zero. Men will have to fight swamps, rivers, ice and cold. Mosquitoes, flies and gnats will not only be annoying but will cause bodily harm. If you are not prepared to work under these and similar conditions DO NOT APPLY.''

Clifton Mon, a staff sergeant assigned to the project, recalls the winter of 1942-1943, when laborers confronted temperatures that plunged to minus 70 degrees Fahrenheit.

"Your breath would turn to ice inside your blankets at night. If you touched anything metal with your bare hands, you couldn't tear your skin loose. We'd have to keep fires burning underneath our trucks all night, or they wouldn't move in the morning."

But few challenges were greater than the engineering dilemma posed by the endless miles of muskeg—expanses of spongy, poorly drained, peatlike organic matter overlying permanently frozen bogs. It took laborers a week or so to learn to leave the muskeg undisturbed and lay down layers of corduroy and gravel to span it. The corduroy was fashioned from thousands upon thousands of logs laid crosswise on top of the muskeg and beneath the roadbed. Each log had to be handcut from the surrounding forests.

Finally, on November 20, 1942, eight months and 12 days after construction began, the road was officially opened. It took another 11 months of work before it was passable year-round. Even then, and for many years after, bridges regularly washed out in the spring and summer months. On one day, July 10, 1943, 40 bridges were swept away.

Today the highway conveys 40,000 vehicles in a normal year. About 90 percent of the highway is paved now, and every year a few more miles of the old dirt road are surfaced, straightened, and otherwise "defanged." The highway is now so tame, most fatalities on the highway can be chalked up to one of two causes: people who run into a moose or fall asleep at the wheel.

A strange little ditty someone scrawled on a bathroom wall along the route that seems to roll on and on forever, describes the Alaskan Highway: "Winding in and winding out / One begins to have some doubts / About the lout who built this route: / Was he going to hell? / Or coming out?[1]

Preparing the Way of the Lord

Although few roads have been as difficult to construct as the Alaskan Highway, trailblazing and road-building are nothing new. In ancient times, Eastern kings returning in triumph from the fields of battle often sent a contingent of men ahead of them to prepare the way for the king and his army. Wherever necessary, they removed any obstacles impeding the king's return. Mountains were leveled, gullies and valleys filled in, crooked roads and trails were straightened, and rough places made as smooth as possible. The quicker this was accomplished, the sooner the nations could see their long-awaited king.

With that thought in mind, consider these verses quoted by John the Baptist in Luke 3:4-6 as the mandate for his ministry:

The voice of one crying in the wilderness: "Prepare the way of the Lord, make His paths straight. Every valley shall be filled and every mountain and hill brought low; and the crooked places shall be made straight and the rough ways smooth; and all flesh shall see the salvation of God" (NKJ).

Obviously, these verses have nothing to do with a highway development program through the Holy Land. The key is found in the fortieth chapter of Isaiah, which contains the original text from which John quoted. The very next verse reads: "Then the glory of the Lord will be revealed, and all flesh will see it together..." (Is. 40:5 NASB).

God not only wants His glory to be revealed to "all flesh" as relating to all the people populating this planet, but I believe this can also mean "all of *my* flesh." God wants His glory to be revealed to every weakness and stronghold in my weak human nature that is so prone to sin and so opposed to the things of God.

Just because my sin has been forgiven does not guarantee that my character and nature have been automatically conformed to the image of Christ. I must examine my heart and my Christian walk, asking, *Are there mountains in my life that are preventing God's glory from being revealed? Are there hills and valleys, rough or crooked places that are impeding the spreading of His message or His appearance?*

Mountains and Hills

Is there anything about your life that has kept God's glory from being revealed to others? Are you a "mountain"—proud, conceited, arrogant, always seeking to promote and exalt yourself? Looming in your character are there mountains and hills of high-mindedness, rebellion, and stubbornness that block the spread of God's glory?

Valleys

Valleys can also present a problem in preparing the way of the Lord. Are you overcome with a sense of unworthiness and failure? Are you bound by inferiority and fear that make you shrink from involvement in both the natural and spiritual realms? Are there low places of loneliness, worry, and despair? Valleys can be so shadowy and dark that very little of the light of God can filter through. Valleys are obstacles to God's glory.

Crookedness

Do you lack integrity, using whatever means are at your disposal to achieve desired ends? Do you testify of salvation with

73

your lips, but live as those who are "crooked" and perverse—like the generation from which you were supposed to be saved? How can God's nature—His glory—be revealed when you live so contrary to His ways?

Roughness

Is your disposition rough and hard? Do you assault others with your sharp words and insensitive actions? Does harshness, rather than kindness, govern your life? Do you speak the truth, but not in love? Do your severity and mercilessness cause others to stumble? Only when your roughness is dealt with can the beauty of the King be revealed through your life.

Reviling, or Revealing?

Christlike character is essential to true godliness. As someone has wisely said, "If character fails, everything fails." To you and me has been given the choice of either reviling or revealing His name.

As the Spirit of the Lord conquers every high and low, every twist and turn in our own fleshly human nature, conforming us to Christ's character and exhibiting His beautiful qualities through us, the glory of the Lord will be revealed through us. Then all those who dwell in darkness around us will be drawn to the Light.

Caution: Highway Under Construction

Lord, I humble myself before You now. Forgive me for the mountains of pride and haughty self-exaltation that block out the rays of Your glory and hinder the winds and life-giving rains of Your Spirit.

It is Your favor and good hand upon my life, O Lord, not my driving, striving labors and perfectionism, that have enabled me to overcome difficulties and enjoy accomplishments and success. **Bring low every mountain, every hill** *of high-mindedness, rebellion, and stubbornness. Demolish every high and lofty thing in my life that sets itself up against the knowledge of You. I must decrease, Lord, and You must increase.*

Dear God, come and **fill the valleys** *in my life. Worry, fear, and feelings of inferiority, like streams trickling through my mind, have cut channels and ravines and valleys into which all my other thoughts are drained. Forgive me for my fear of failure, my despair and depression, my lack of trust in Your unwavering faithfulness.*

Forgive me for attempting to fill the lonely, empty places in my life with anything but Your presence and Your divine purposes for me. Teach me to cast all my cares upon You. Come, God, and fill the valleys.

Whatever it takes, please **make straight the crooked places** *in my life, Father. Forgive my twisting of truth, my distortions of reality, my moral crookedness, my warped priorities and values. In times of temptation, help me always to choose a good name and the straight and right way, rather than riches or favor gained by devious, crooked means.*

Make the rough places smooth, dear Lord. Balance the uneven places in my nature. Smooth and fill the personality "pot holes" that cause unexpected jolts to those around me, disrupting harmony and progress. Remove those things in my life that are causing me to be a stumbling block to others. Help me to stop blaming and criticizing everyone else, and to set to work on my own rough places instead. May Christ be fully formed in me. May I be wholly conformed to His image. May Your glory be revealed in **all** *my flesh.*

Father, from this moment on, may the all-consuming reason for my existence be that all those around me might see the beauty of Jesus in me and the glory of His salvation. Amen.

Endnotes

1. John Krakauer, "Ice, Mosquitos and Muskeg—Building the Road to Alaska," *Smithsonian* (July 1992), pp. 102-110.

Section Two

Preparing for Ministry

Chapter Seven

The Birthing of a Ministry

"No birth, no pregnancy, no conception!"

God is looking for men and women...

Who fear nothing but God.
Who are totally committed to God, regardless of what others think or say.
Who desire, above everything else, an intimacy with the Lord.
Who long to know Him, regardless of the cost.
Who are prepared to break with tradition for the sake of obedience.
Who won't sell out to fame or fortune.
Who have died to carnal ambitions.
Who no longer measure their success by the world's standards.

God is looking for men and women of maturity....

But there is no maturity because there is no birth.
There is no birth because there is no pregnancy.
There is no pregnancy because there is no conception.

There is no conception because there is no intimate relationship.
There is no intimate relationship because we busy ourselves seeking satisfaction apart from God.

Requirements for Birthing a Godly Ministry

In every generation God desires to raise up men and women who will be instruments for His purpose. Invariably, His instruments are unique. They don't usually conform to the status quo. They bear the distinctive markings "made by God"!

How is such a ministry born? What is the birth process like, if a ministry is to be truly God's creation? The story of the birth of Samson, told in Judges 13, provides some lessons regarding the birthing of a ministry.

For 40 years, Israel had been under Philistine rule. Because of Israel's sins, God had handed the nation over to their enemies. Their circumstances gave them no hope. Their morale was gone; their resistance was low; they had nothing to do but submit to their conquerors and allow the Philistines a free hand.

As happens so often, man had come to the end of his resources and reached the point of desperation: then God stepped in. The Angel of the Lord appeared to a woman and her husband, Manoah, who were childless. A new ministry was about to be birthed, and God selected as His instrument a woman who was barren.

Acknowledging Our Barrenness

God's first requirement in ministry is barrenness. God looks for people who are incapable of producing life on their own— those who have come to the end of their own striving and honestly admit their true condition. Most of us, not wanting to bear this reproach, go around feigning "life." Our activities become the substitute for the anointing. Programs replace productivity and prayer. Life seems to abound everywhere, until one looks below the surface and realizes it's only a veneer—a form of godliness that lacks power.

Why does God insist on barrenness as a prerequisite for blessing? Simply because no flesh can glory in it. If David, after his success with Goliath, had been clothed in Saul's armor, no doubt Saul would have claimed some of the credit. God has to strip us first so that He alone is glorified.

Opening the Womb

God promised Manoah's wife that, even though she was barren, she would conceive and bear a son. Here, then, lies the second requirement of a God-birthed ministry: God has to "open the womb." This is beyond our own capability. Having reached the point of desperation and honesty, we can now cry out for God to touch us.

If the Lord answered the desperate longings of Manoah's wife, as well as the cries of Sarah, Hannah, Ruth, Rebekah, Rachel, and Elizabeth, surely He can release us in the same way.

Bringing About Conception

Conception is only possible after commitment. God demands preeminence in our lives; we must put the Lord above all other loves. Only when we come to Him in undivided love can conception take place. Our determination to pursue any other love that competes for preeminence—whether it be sports, fashion, successful church programs, career goals, or financial prosperity—violates our relationship with God.

Conception takes place alone with your beloved. Conception is a private matter, reserved for the couple alone. So, likewise, in the spiritual, God draws us aside and shuts us in with Himself, away from the crowd. There, in quiet isolation from distracting activities, He reveals Himself to us.

Conception requires nakedness. Everything must be exposed before conception takes place. We must be willing to be seen for who we are. So often we seek to cover ourselves, trying to maintain an image of strength and self-sufficiency. But before God, we must be vulnerable, exposing the weaknesses and sins that beset us.

Honesty before God is essential for conception. We see that truth operating in the life of King David, who had to be open before God before he was restored. In Psalm 51, he bares his true condition to God and receives cleansing.

Conception should take place out of a loving relationship. As we spend time with God, a loving atmosphere is created in which conception can take place. As we love Him with all our heart, soul, mind, and strength, our time with the Lord becomes a delightful and refreshing experience. As with a natural relationship, time and place make no difference. Love always finds a way.

Guarding and Growing

Following conception comes gestation. This is the time in which the ministry is hidden, but the growth process has begun. Something is being developed. Unseen by the natural eye, changes begin to take place. So also in the spiritual sense, certain changes begin. This is a critical time—caution must be taken in order to protect what has been committed to us.

Manoah's wife was told that she must be careful. She was asked to refrain from those things which might contaminate her body. Three times she was warned not to eat any unclean thing or to drink wine or strong drink. Not being a Nazarite herself, why did God require this of her? The reason becomes apparent when we understand that her son Samson was called of God from the womb to be a Nazarite. How then could she give birth to something she wasn't prepared to be herself? Imagine as the boy grew, if while telling him to refrain from certain things, she sat next to him eating and drinking. What kind of example would that have been?

The principle is clear: We cannot minister to others what we have not received ourselves. An individual can't effectively minister on holiness unless he or she personally desires and pursues holiness. How tragic when a Christian leader, after writing articles and books on marriage, is reported to be in the process of a divorce. Effectiveness is destroyed unless the quality of one's life matches the quality of one's ministry.

Bringing to Birth

After months of concealment, the birth process finally begins. But pain and labor are required to bring forth life. Remember how Paul talks about those who "work hard" at ministry and how the apostle likens himself to being in labor until Christ is formed in His people? No one enjoys pain, yet it is necessary in the birthing process.

Providing Constant Care

Birth is but the beginning. After birth, there is the need to provide constant care. But we need training to be effective caretakers. When Manoah's wife received the promise of a child, she also entreated God for instructions on how to raise him.

In our excitement of birthing a ministry, we can easily forget to ask God for wisdom on how to maintain it. Some have given birth to genuine, godly ministries, but have watched them die because they neglected to rely upon God's instruction.

The story of Samson shows how a great ministry came to a halt because of failure to seek God's direction. Samson lost his freedom, his sight, his testimony, his anointing, his strength, and his respect—all because he lost contact with God.

Barrenness or Blessing?

The Church desperately needs men and women of maturity who are anointed and empowered by God and willing to allow the Holy Spirit to fulfill His purposes through them.

God's problem today is not the strength of the enemy, but the weakness of the Church. Why is it that throughout Scripture man is never portrayed as being barren—only woman? Because the woman is a type of the Church. The failure is never on God's side, but on ours.

So, if you're barren, reach out to the Source of life.

He makes the barren woman "a joyful mother of children" (Ps. 113:9 NKJ).

Through you, God will birth a unique ministry. From your life will flow great blessing and benefit to others.

Chapter Eight

Lessons on Leadership

I'm convinced the Church stands on the threshold of a new outpouring of God's Spirit. We've entered a time of transition. The call to move forward is being sounded once again. We are seeing an unprecedented shaking—which is destroying everything not firmly rooted in the bedrock of Jesus Christ. And in the midst of all this, God is preparing a new breed of leadership that will equip the Church for its next role.

We are in a time not unlike that described in the beginning of the Book of Joshua. It was a time of transition for the nation of Israel. Their 40 years of wanderings had finally ended, marking the end of an era under the leadership of their great statesman, Moses. God announced to Joshua that he was to lead the nation into the next phase of His divine purpose.

The book begins with the Lord telling Joshua, "Moses My servant is dead... (Josh. 1:2)." This was not simply a natural occurrence, but a tragic event which Moses brought on himself.

We're told in Deuteronomy that when Moses died he was in excellent physical condition. "His eye was not dim nor his vigor abated" (Deut. 34:7b). I believe the reason behind Moses' untimely death can help shed some light on what we are seeing happening in the body of Christ today. Let me remind you that "all these things that were written aforetime were for our instruction" (see Rom. 15:4).

Moses, a Mighty Man of God

God had given Moses the awesome task of leading His people into the Promised Land. No one, apart from Christ Himself, can compare with the qualities that are revealed in Moses' character. His willingness to lay down his life for the sheep, notably his patience with the large company of murmurers, was exemplary. Added to this, we have the record of his intimate encounters with the Lord. Again and again we see him inquiring of God for direction, eager to know the next move and refusing to rely on his own understanding. After Moses' early years in the palace of Pharaoh and his subsequent call to leadership, we are told little about any defects in his character. But Numbers 20 describes the one mistake that prompted Moses' untimely dismissal as a leader and the withdrawal of the privilege of being one who would possess the land.

A Grave Mistake

Israel had arrived at Kadesh only to find that they had no water. Rather than seeking for a godly solution to the problem, the people chose to rebel against Moses and Aaron. Moses fell on his face before God seeking an answer to this dilemma. Suddenly the glory of the Lord appeared, and Moses was instructed to take his rod, assemble all the congregation and "...speak to the rock before their eyes, that it may yield its water..." (Num. 20:8). But Moses vented his anger with the people by striking the rock twice instead of speaking to it as God had commanded.

God, true to His promise, brought forth an abundance of water, enough for all the people as well as their flocks and herds. But then God turned His attention to Moses and Aaron, informing them that their time as leaders was over and that neither of them would see the fulfillment of His purpose in bringing Israel into the land. Moses was commanded to take Aaron to the top of Mount Hor, strip him of his garments (his divine office) and place them on Aaron's son Eleazar.

Moses now faced the task of leading the people alone. Aaron had been removed from office, and Moses had had his sentence deferred. He was to lead the nation with the knowledge that ultimately he would die in the wilderness because of his disobedient, angry outburst.

The Scripture records Moses' reaction to this rather severe penalty:

> *"I also pleaded with the Lord at that time, saying... 'Let me, I pray, cross over and see the fair land that is beyond the Jordan....' But the Lord was angry with me on your account, and would not listen to me; and the Lord said to me, 'Enough! Speak to Me no more of this matter'"* (Deuteronomy 3:23-26).

God permitted Moses to climb to the top of Mount Pisgah to view the Promised Land, but not without reminding Moses again that he could not cross the Jordan. Moses had to live with the knowledge that because of his anger and disobedience, he had forfeited the blessing of being part of God's next great move.

As the time drew to a close, God spoke to Moses giving him direction: "Then the Lord said to Moses, 'Behold, the time for you to die is near; call Joshua, and present yourself at the tent of meeting, that I may commission him.'..." (Deut. 31:14).

Moses then gave his final word of exhortation to God's people, warning them that they were to carefully observe all the words of God's law. "For it is not an idle word for you; indeed it is your life. And by this word you shall prolong your days..." (Deut. 32:47). Moses' own life demonstrated this principle at work. He had disobeyed the word of the Lord, only to find that his life was shortened as a consequence.

Israel watched as Moses, in obedience to God's command, climbed Mount Nebo, never to return.

And the Lord spoke to Moses that very same day, saying, "Go up to this mountain...Then die on the mountain where you ascend...because you broke faith with Me in the midst of the sons of Israel...because you did not treat Me as holy in the midst of the sons of Israel. For you shall see the land at a distance, but you shall not go there..." (Deuteronomy 32:48-52).

Here God fully revealed the reason for His displeasure against Moses with the words, "because you did not treat Me as holy in the midst of Israel."

God's Displeasure With Leaders

I'm convinced that we're seeing God's dealings with Moses repeated today as a sign of God's displeasure with His leaders. All around us ministries are being shaken and leaders are being dismissed from power and positions of authority. Their death, by whatever means it comes (physical, financial, or spiritual), is the end result of leaders who have not treated God as holy before the people. God's standard for leadership has always been higher than the standard required of the average believer; therefore, His judgment for leaders is also greater.

Joshua, God's Servant

Now that Moses was gone, who would lead Israel into her inheritance?

Now it came about after the death of Moses the servant of the Lord that the Lord spoke to Joshua the son of Nun, Moses' servant, saying, "Moses My servant is dead [Why? Because I took him]*; now therefore arise, cross this Jordan, you and all this people..."* (Joshua 1:1-2).

The leadership vacuum resulting from Moses' death didn't take God by surprise. Joshua had long been under God's scrutiny. God had been preparing His man and had him waiting in the wings.

Imagine having to "fill the sandals" of Moses, the mighty man of God who led Israel out of Egyptian bondage, established them as an independent nation, and prepared the Israelites for entrance into Canaan. What qualities do we find in Joshua that equipped him for such an awesome responsibility?

Gaining Victory Over Sin

Joshua first appears prominently in the Scriptures when Moses chose him to lead Israel's army against the Amalekites. The significance of that battle is often overlooked. The Amalekites, referred to as "the sinners, the Amalekites" (1 Sam. 15:18 NKJ) were seeking to bring about the downfall of God's people. This was a battle against sin and the flesh, and Joshua gained the victory. That victory marked the beginning of his rise to leadership. It also reveals an important quality that helped qualify Joshua for leadership. Joshua refused to allow sin and the flesh to gain dominion over him. He was determined to gain victory over sin.

Today, as in Joshua's day, God is looking for those who are living in victory over sin and the flesh. Those who, rather than surrendering to sin and self, are prepared to fight until they conquer. But how is that battle won?

The battle Joshua led was won not simply by the force of numbers or by mere human effort. Victory came because as Joshua was fighting in the valley, Moses was interceding on the mountain. In other words, the real key to overcoming sin is understanding that we are powerless in our strength; our victory comes by maintaining contact with the power of God. (See Exodus 17:8-13.)

Patiently Awaiting God's Timing

The second glimpse into Joshua's life is found in Exodus 24. Moses, called by God to come up the mountain, takes Joshua with him. For the next 40 days Israel is left under the command of Aaron. It would appear that, having ascended part way up the mountain with Moses, Joshua is left behind, while Moses ascends further and is enveloped in the cloud. During this 40-day period, the Israelites become impatient and take things into their own hands, producing the golden calf. The entire nation, from Aaron down, become involved in this apostasy. Only Joshua, patiently awaiting Moses' return with a fresh word from God for the people, is exempt.

The question this story presents to us is this: Are we willing to await God's timing, or do we become impatient and produce our own "gods"? How difficult is it to be patient with God's timetable? Like Abraham, we seek to fulfill His promises quickly, only to produce an "Ishmael" in the end. How desperately we, like Joshua, need to have patience in the things of God!

Lingering in God's Presence

Exodus 33 gives us the third important principle in Joshua's development: He knew what it was to spend time with God.

While Moses sought God concerning Israel's idolatry, we are told that young Joshua "...would not depart from the tent..." of meeting (Ex. 33:11). Here was a young man hungry for the presence of God, a man who willingly remained in the tent for the sole purpose of being with God.

Many believers today, even those in leadership, spend little time with the Lord. No wonder we are seeing men falling like tenpins, unaware of their spiritual bankruptcy. The next move of God will be led by believers who know their God, for they "...shall be strong, and do exploits" (Dan. 11:32 KJV).

Letting Faith Arise

The fourth leadership quality we see in Joshua is his faith. Chosen as one of the spies, he experienced firsthand the first fruits of Israel's inheritance. Convinced that entering the long-awaited Promised Land was God's purpose for everyone, Joshua sought to encourage the people to believe God's word. But the response to his encouragement was unbelief, including the sneers and loudly voiced fears of ten other leaders who spied out the land with him. (See Numbers 13–14.)

Today we are seeing the faith of Joshua arise in the hearts of God's people who desperately desire more of Him. Many times these victorious voices in the wilderness are met with opposition from people who, like Israel of old, "despise the pleasant land" (see Ps. 106:24). But once again we will see God raise up a new generation of people who will stop at nothing to fulfill His purposes and enter into their full inheritance.

Developing a Serving Spirit

The fifth lesson we learn from this remarkable man was his serving spirit. Nowhere do we see Joshua striving for position or being critical of Moses' leadership. Several times the Scriptures draw attention to the fact that Joshua was a servant. At Joshua's death, recorded in Joshua 24:29, he is referred to as "Joshua, the son of Nun, the servant of the Lord." Joshua served Moses; he served his nation; he served his God.

How unlike Joshua's spirit is the contemporary emphasis on dominion and the teaching that man's destiny is rulership rather than servanthood. Jesus said the greatest among you must become servant of all. In modern language, "the way up is down," for the lowly and meek will inherit the earth.

One of the characteristics of God's next move will be a new leadership style. The self-serving demigods have had their day. I believe God is now requiring men and women like Joshua, who are willing to pour out their lives in order that those they lead may be blessed and empowered to fulfill God's purposes.

Possessing a Shepherd's Heart

A sixth quality that fitted Joshua for leadership was a shepherd's heart. Moses, conscious of the fact that his time was coming to an end, asked God to appoint a man over the congregation who would lead them so they would not be "like sheep which have no shepherd" (see Num. 27:16-20). God responded to this by telling Moses to appoint Joshua for the task.

One of the great cries today throughout the body of Christ is for shepherds who care for the flock and are willing to lay down their lives for the sheep; shepherds prepared to defend the flock from wolves; shepherds who know their sheep by name.

Unlike the shepherd, the hireling is concerned with his own interests. He performs a task, not because of his love for the sheep, but for the sake of gain. Recent financial disclosures have exposed lavish spending among some leaders in ministry whose flocks are constantly being fleeced to provide for the shepherd. May God deliver His people from hireling-hearted leaders. And may God give us shepherds like Joshua whose supreme joy springs from their relationship with the great Shepherd and their love for the flock!

Leadership Lessons

Let's take a moment to review the important principles we've gleaned from the lives of Moses and Joshua, two of God's choicest servants:

1. Failure to carefully observe all that God tells us to do can result in the shortening of our lives and the forfeiting of our ministries and places of leadership.

2. God is looking for leaders who, refusing to surrender to the enemies of sin and the flesh, draw power from His might, then fight until they conquer.

3. Godly leaders know the secret of waiting for God's timing rather than growing impatient and producing their own "gods."

4. The next move of God will be led by believers who, like Moses and Joshua, take time to linger in the presence of God.

5. Successful leaders focus their faith upon God, His purposes, and His promises rather than upon giants and reasoned analysis contradicting God's clear command.

6. Servanthood is "in"; self-serving demigods are "out."

7. The supreme joy of a true shepherd springs out of relationship with the great Shepherd and love for the sheep, not from financial gain that comes from fleecing the flock.

The leadership of Moses and Joshua provides lessons for every believer desiring to develop in maturity and minister effectively as a beloved, faithful servant of God.

Chapter Nine

Three Critical Issues on the Road to Maturity

As we progress in our walk with God, three key issues emerge. They are: (a) How we regard ourselves; (b) How we regard change, and (c) How we regard God. If we're to continue the process of moving on to spiritual adulthood, it's critical that we learn to deal with these issues properly.

Abraham, whose story unfolds in chapters 11 through 25 of Genesis, successfully confronted each of these critical issues. Because Abraham is called the father of all who believe (see Rom. 4:11) and is held up as an example of faith at its best, you and I can learn a great deal by studying Abraham's attitude toward himself, toward change, and toward God.

Dealing With Self

Abraham's attitude toward himself seems to be symbolized by an object that was continually present in his life: the altar. During turning points and times of major decision in his life, we see this dedicated man building altars (see Gen. 12:7-8; 13:4,18; 22:9).

Altars played a leading role in all Old Testament worship of the true God. Their importance is seen in the fact that the word *altar* is used 433 times in the Bible (KJV).

Most of the altars were built for sacrificial purposes, but some seem to have been memorials (see Ex. 17:15-16; Josh. 22:26-27). But in addition to the altar for sacrifice, we also are an altar for incense. The burning of incense upon this altar symbolized the offering up of the believer's prayers (see Rev. 8:3). (Interestingly, it was while Zacharias was officiating at this altar that an angel appeared, revealing that a son [John the Baptist] would be born to this aging priest and his wife. See Luke 1:8-13.)

As we've just seen in our brief study, an altar could be a memorial or it could be a place of sacrifice, intercession, communion, consecration, or revelation. At the altar, the believer met with God.

The lack of an altar in the life of a child of God speaks of one who knows little of God's true nature. For example, King Saul, whose life was filled with disobedience, instability, and tragedy, was 42 years old, king of Israel, and had a grown son before he ever built his first altar (see 1 Sam. 14:35).

But for Abraham, the altar was where he laid down his life before the Lord, inquiring of Him and requiring God's presence and favor as his most vital necessity. Through a lifetime of building altars and dedicating himself to do the Lord's will, Abraham had come to understand and trust God's character and nature.

Understanding Who God Is

Like Abraham, we begin the process of laying down our lives at the altar as we begin understanding who God is. Revelation produces consecration.

Revelation also produces obedience. Abraham had learned that the altar, representing submission and self-sacrifice, was put in his life for his good, not for his destruction. Because he trusted and was intimately acquainted with God, Abraham was not afraid to obey Him, even when God proved and tested His servant by commanding Abraham to place his only son Isaac, whom he loved, on an altar and slay him (see Gen. 22:2).

His instant, unquestioning obedience to God's command exposed Abraham's attitude toward himself. Abraham embraced the altar. God was Lord and Master; Abraham was His humble, obedient servant. If His all-wise and trustworthy Master asked him to sacrifice the son who meant more to him than life itself, Abraham would not hold Isaac back or begrudge giving him to God (see Gen. 22:12). If his God required such worship, then Abraham would embrace the altar of sacrifice and offer that worship, even through tears. How precious, how sobering, to realize that although God did not require Abraham to give his only son, the time came when God Himself gave His (see Jn. 3:16).

Submission or Self-Preservation?

Our immediate, instinctive reaction to the altar of self-sacrifice is resistance, for everything within the human spirit seeks to hold onto life. Each of us possesses a strong instinct for self-preservation. We see this in the amazing stories of heroism produced by the will to survive. We read of hikers trapped for days in a raging blizzard at subzero temperatures who somehow manage to emerge from the ordeal alive. We hear stories of prisoners of war who, when being starved by their captors, resorted to desperate measures—like eating bugs, rodents, or even worse—to keep from dying.

For example, Father Lawrence Martin Jenco and David Jacobsen, who were held hostage in Lebanon for more than one and a half years, tell of being served a favorite dish they called "hint of chicken," meaning that the chicken had quite recently walked through their rice. Even the thought makes our stomachs revolt, but for hungry hostages who desperately desired to live, that detestable dish provided much-needed nourishment.

The love of life carries over into the spiritual realm as well. As believers, we mistakenly seek to "save our lives" no matter what the cost. Our immediate reaction to the altar is resistance, for everything within us seeks to hold onto life.

We soon discover, however, that the more we fight, the less we have; the very thing we seek to gain, we lose. Jesus laid out this principle in His call to discipleship:

> *...If any one desires to be My disciple, let him deny himself— that is, disregard, lose sight of and forget himself and his own interests—and take up his cross and follow Me [cleave steadily to Me, conform wholly to My example in living and if need be in dying, also]. For whoever is bent on saving his [temporal] life [his comfort and security here], shall lose [eternal life]; and whoever loses his life [his comfort and security here] for My sake, shall find [life everlasting]* (Matthew 16:24-25 AMP).

Although the greatest temptation to the believer is to "come down from the cross and save yourself," the only people God can use are the "dead" ones. We must be willing to decrease in order that He might increase.

Keeping Our Commitments

Once we begin the process of laying down our lives at the altar, we must not go back on our commitments. We see this principle in the law of the burnt offering (see Lev. 6:9). The sacrifice was to remain on the altar all night, and the fire was to be kept burning. However, sometimes in the night seasons of our lives we are tempted to let the fire go out and remove ourselves from the altar. During our long nights of testing, we must remember and keep the vows we have made to God.

Building Our Altars God's Way

When we, like Abraham, build an altar to God, we must also be careful to do it His way, not ours. As we see in Exodus 20:24-26, God gave specific instructions concerning the altars the Israelites could make to Him. First, an altar was to be constructed of either earth or stone. The stones were not to be cut or engraved in any way; to do so was to profane the altar, making the sacrifice unacceptable.

This instruction was given because the altar was not to draw attention to itself because of its beauty; nor was it to glorify the one who created it. The danger for those who have once surrendered their lives to the Lord is that we're tempted to glory in our own righteousness—whether it be our upright lifestyle, consistent prayer life or Bible reading, or the success of our ministry. In the midst of "sacrificing" we can become like the Pharisee who stood in the temple extolling his virtues (see Lk. 18:9-14). The altar in his life constituted nothing more than the worship of self.

Second, the altar was not to have any steps. An altar to the holy God was not to resemble the altars built by the heathen nations to their gods, for their worship often revolved around the sensual realm. Steps were built up to these altars so that as the priest or priestess ascended, their nakedness was exposed through their loose-flowing robes. The higher the priest ascended, the more flesh was revealed. This, in turn, aroused sexual frenzy among the people.

In prohibiting the use of steps ascending to His altar, God was teaching His people two important principles. First, the flesh is not to be exhibited, but destroyed. Second, we cannot please God by our attempts at raising or exalting ourselves. If we are not careful, our "altars" can become a place to exalt the flesh rather than the place to crucify it.

Dying to Self

Through his long, intimate relationship with the Lord, Abraham had come to know his God. Abraham had also come to know his own weak, failure-prone self. Abraham had learned not to hold anything back from God, for he knew that the altar, even when it meant the ultimate sacrifice, was put in his life for his good, not for his destruction.

Did you ever wonder why Paul, in writing to the Romans, takes 11 chapters to talk about the "mercies of God" before exhorting the believers to present their bodies as a living sacrifice? I think I know at least one reason. Only as we become increasingly aware of God's beauty and holiness, only as we, like Abraham, get to know our Lord's character and nature, do we long to be like Him. Only then do we long to give ourselves wholly to Him. And only then are we prepared to die to self that Christ might be seen in us.

Dealing With Change

The attitude Abraham exhibited toward change is also instructive. God's first command to Abraham required change: "Get thee out of thy father's house" (see Gen. 12:1). The house, the residence in which one abides, the place to which one returns, suggests security. A house represents that which is permanent, immovable.

In the life of the believer, the "house" can constitute the greatest obstacle to change. All of us are creatures of habit. We feel comfortable in familiar surroundings, following a routine. No one enjoys being dislodged.

The Book of Hebrews speaks of Abraham as a sojourner, one whose life was one of continual change. Imagine the ramifications of that lifestyle.

By faith he dwelt in the land of promise as in a foreign country, dwelling in tents with Isaac and Jacob, the heirs with him of the same promise; for he waited for the city which has foundations, whose builder and maker is God (Hebrews 11:9-10 NKJ).

Abraham was a tent dweller. While a house suggests permanency, a tent represents transition, flexibility, progression, freedom. Abraham is depicted in Hebrews as someone who was continually moving, searching, looking. God desires to build this dynamic within us, that we might be a seeking people. God desires people whose "hearts are the highways to Zion," people who find security and permanence in eternal things, rather than in clinging to that which is temporal.

One of the Church's biggest handicaps today is its resistance to change. Unlike the sojourning spirit that Abraham modeled for us, we tend to enjoy building houses and settling down. We resist God's prodding to move on into unfamiliar territory. Instead of clinging to the Lord, we cling to the truths that have brought us this far. For the Baptist, it's baptism; for those in the Holiness movement, it's sanctification; for the Pentecostals, it's spiritual gifts. Nothing is wrong with these truths, but if we cling to our "pet" doctrines instead of embracing God's revealed truth in its full, balanced entirety, we will be hindered from possessing new ground that God wants to give us.

Take, for example, the story of Israel. You recall that while in the wilderness they grew tired of their food and circumstances. Consequently, God chastened them by sending serpents among them. Later, when in response to Moses' intercession, God gave them deliverance in the form of a brazen serpent, many were those who rejoiced in God's provision. Whole generations later recalled how, if it hadn't been for the brazen serpent, all their forefathers would have been wiped out in God's wrath.

Yet the blessing of the brazen serpent soon became a bondage to the very people it blessed. During the reign of Hezekiah, hundreds of years later, that same brazen serpent had become an object of worship, Israel's favorite idol (see 2 Kings 18:4). The very object that was to testify of God became a god, an idol. Likewise, for the Pharisees, the very Scriptures that were to point them to Christ, became their obstacle to Christ.

> *Jesus said, "You search and investigate and pore over the Scriptures diligently, because you suppose and trust that you have eternal life through them. And these [very Scriptures] testify about Me! And still you are not willing (but refuse) to come to Me, so that you might have life"* (John 5:39-40 AMP).

Today fundamentalists, like the Pharisees, are in danger of becoming so focused on the written word that the Living Word is bound in their midst. No religious group, no individual believer, is exempt from the temptation to stop at a cherished place of blessing and settle into a comfortable theology or structure rather than moving deeper into the territory that God has promised and longs to provide.

We need to ask ourselves continually: Am I living in a house or in a tent? Am I going back to the place of familiarity and security, or am I ever conquering and claiming new spiritual frontiers?

Dealing With God

Abraham also is a model for us in his attitude toward God Himself. The Scriptures say Isaac dug again the wells of his father, Abraham (see Gen. 26:18). Wells are a recurring symbol in the Word of God. A cistern is merely for storing water, and a spring is found at the surface. But a well is dug in the earth down to the water table, the level at which the ground is permanently saturated with water. Well water is cool, refreshing, but most of all, fresh.

Jeremiah, lamenting the condition of Israel's decline, said that God's people were guilty of two grievous evils (see Jer. 2:13). First, they had forsaken the One who was the fountain of living water. Second, they were drinking from cisterns of their own making. He later speaks of their drinking from the waters of the Nile and Euphrates (see Jer. 2:18). How could people whom God intended to find their satisfaction in Him end up drinking from the waters of Egypt and Assyria, heathen nations that sought to dominate and oppress Israel? How could God's people look to Egypt, a type of the earthbound system called "the world," to quench their thirst?

Professing Christians can slip into the same practice, finding more satisfaction in the world than they do in Christ. As believers desiring to press on to spiritual adulthood, we need to drink deeply from God's well. We need to spend less time reading the sports page and more time reading the Word of God. We need to cultivate our desire for God, praying that we might be thirsty in our spirits, until we would rather spend an hour in His presence than an hour in front of the television. God wants us to find more satisfaction and enjoyment in the house of God, worshiping and fellowshipping with His people, than we get cheering for our favorite team in the sports stadium.

Far too often, God's people rely upon the polluted puddles and shallow streams of the world to quench their thirst. But puddles and streams disappear in times of drought. Desperate, desolate days of drought are on the horizon. Begin now to dig into the deep things of God where the ground is permanently saturated with the waters of God's presence, power, and provision.

An old Chinese proverb says, "Dig the well before you are thirsty." Believers who are wise will hear and take heed. Our survival may depend upon it.

From what source are you drinking? Jesus still cries out: "If any man thirst, let him come unto Me, and drink" (Jn. 7:37b KJV). Nothing else satisfies.

Facing Three Critical Issues

As we reach for spiritual adulthood, let's be Abrahams in our outlook. First, let's not shrink back from laying our lives on the altar; let's die to our selfish ways that we might gain new life in Christ. Second, let's welcome change in our lives—especially in our understanding of Scripture and the ways of God. Instead of clinging only to the familiarity of long-held religious doctrines, let's be willing to pull up the tent stakes and keep moving forward in God. Finally, let's not try to satisfy our thirsty souls with worldly pursuits that will only leave us wanting. Rather, let's be like Abraham and dig a well that will satisfy us with the water of life.

Chapter Ten

Instructions for Believers as Kings

Even before anyone came, there were amazing events: a comet appeared and split into three; the waters of the lake boiled up in a rage; a sign like a tongue of fire burned up into the sky, up to the heavens.

These and other remarkable things began to happen ten years before the Spaniards landed: omens that foretold their coming, said the old men who drew pictographs of them some 30 years afterward for a Franciscan missionary.

According to the missionary's aged informants, a messenger brought word of "towers or small mountains floating on the waves of the sea." The ships came in the spring of 1519, off the northern shore of the Yucatan peninsula. Hernando Cortes, a soldier of fortune, led the Spaniards who, with their white skin, suits of armor, cannons, and horses, were an arresting sight.

Cortes informed the Indians who came to greet him that he wanted to see Montezuma, the emperor of the 25-million-strong

Aztec empire in central Mexico, stretching from the Gulf Coast to the Pacific Ocean, and as far south as present-day Guatemala.

Cortes asked the Indians if Montezuma had any gold. When informed that he did, Cortes said, in a phrase that has rung down through the ages, "Send me some of it, because I and my companions suffer from a disease of the heart which can be cured only with gold."

In reply, Montezuma sent extremely lavish gifts to Cortes, saying that Cortes should determine what he needed for himself and "the cure for his sickness," but that a meeting between Cortes and the emperor would be impossible.

Undismayed, Cortes set out to Montezuma's capital, the present site of Mexico City, to see the emperor. As he made his way through various villages and city-states, Cortes stirred up uprising among embittered Indians who had been subjugated by Montezuma.

As they approached the Aztec capital, the Spaniards set foot on a causeway—wide enough for ten horsemen to ride abreast. Partway along it, they were met by 4,000 richly dressed gentlemen of the court who bowed to the Spaniards as a sign of peace. Then, just across a little bridge, the Spaniards saw Montezuma, walking under a pallium of gold and green feathers, strung about with silver hangings, and carried by four men. He was supported on the arms of two royal princes.

Courtiers walked ahead of Montezuma, sweeping the ground and laying down thin mantles so that his feet never touched the earth. The emperor ordered that Cortes and many of his Indian allies be shown to a beautiful palace and left alone for a time.

The city, built up atop mudbanks and islands and laced with canals and bridges, was a wonder of human artifice. Three long, wide causeways connected it to the mainland, and an aqueduct brought fresh water from a hillside spring into the middle of the city. More than 60,000 people came daily to the marketplace to buy and sell a vast array of goods.

All around the city were many beautiful temples, but Cortes later told of one "whose great size and magnificence no human tongue could describe." The main temple occupied a site about 70 by 80 yards at its base, with two staircases leading up nearly 200 feet to a terrace and twin shrines. There the stones were splattered black with the blood of *human sacrifices.*

It was a gruesome procedure. After a priest had cut the victim open, reached in and plucked out his still-beating heart, offering it up in a sacred vessel, often to placate the sun, the body was thrown down the temple steps, flayed, and cut up. Its skull went to a great skull rack where it is said there were 136,000 skulls, arranged in rows, and the remainder of the body was sometimes ceremoniously eaten, usually by the warriors who had captured the victim.

As it began to dawn on the Spaniards that there was no reason for Montezuma to let them leave the city alive, eventually they devised a plan to seize Montezuma and hold him hostage in his own city, in the same way that Montezuma customarily held numerous rival chiefs as permanent hostages.

Eventually, perhaps to quench the Spanish thirst for gold, Montezuma agreed not only to open up his personal treasure but to call in gifts from his whole empire and give them to Cortes. It is said there was so much gold from Montezuma's gifts alone, it took the Spaniards three days to examine it.

Just as some of the Aztec leaders began telling Montezuma that either the Spaniards should leave or the Aztecs should kill them, messengers brought word that 18 more Spanish ships with 900 soldiers had been spotted where Cortes had originally landed. Sensing the presence of rivals for the Aztec riches and a possible split among the Spaniards, Cortes left for the coast, leaving fewer than 100 soldiers behind.

Taking the other Spanish captain and his army by surprise at night, Cortes put the captain in irons. Most of his men joined Cortes, including a Negro sick with the smallpox.

Back in the capital city, however, violence had exploded when the Spanish soldiers Cortes had left behind waded into the midst of Indians celebrating an annual festival in the courtyard of the great temple square, beheading, stabbing, and spearing without mercy. When the Aztecs counterattacked, full-scale fighting swept through the city. The powerless emperor watched as the city was threatened with disaster.

Hearing the news, Cortes rushed back to the city, discovering along the way that all the land was in revolt. Once inside the city, Cortes and his men found themselves surrounded and attacked by angry enemy warriors. At last Cortes sent for Montezuma and asked him to go up to the roof of the palace and tell his people to stop the fighting and allow the Spaniards to leave in peace. But Montezuma was wounded while appealing to the crowd, and soon thereafter, died in Spanish hands.

The Spaniards, attempting to flee the city, found that the Aztecs had destroyed many of the bridges. Trying to get over the breaks and gaps without bridges was a disaster as their horses slipped and fell into the water, cannon and bundles and boxes following. Those Spaniards who had been most greedy about stuffing gold into their clothes were among the first to sink with the weight of it as they crossed, so "those who died, died rich."

Cortes and the men who escaped eventually regrouped, destroyed the aqueduct bringing the main supply of fresh water into the city, and then began the three-month siege that brought about the city's collapse.

As the Spaniards walked at last down the inner streets of the conquered city, they tied handkerchiefs over their noses to guard against the stench. Among the piles of bodies were people who had died not so much of wounds as of starvation and of various diseases, especially smallpox—the virus that had made its way across Mexico with Cortes' army.

Cortes went on to great wealth and power. But in the end, accused of murder and mismanagement, he died brokenhearted in Spain. Smallpox and other epidemics spread throughout the Aztec empire, subsiding and recurring, until eventually, of a total population of perhaps 25 million, as many as 22 million died. And with them died the Aztec civilization…a sobering testimony to what men with power, but no character, can do.[1]

As we are about to see in our study, power, fueled by lust and greed, is a dangerous, deadly thing. That is why God demands strict adherence to His high standards and principles from those who lead others—especially those who lead in His name.

A Twofold Function

From the beginning, God created man to have a twofold spiritual function—that of king and priest. This calling can be traced from Genesis to Revelation (see Ex. 19:3,6; 1 Pet. 2:5,9; Rev. 5:10). The function of the king was to be governmental; the function of the priest, sacrificial and mediatory.

God created mankind to rule. Adam and Eve not only shared communion with God, but they also were to have dominion with

God and over everything God had created. Their divine mandate was to subdue the earth. Through relationship they were granted rulership.

However, when Adam and Eve yielded to the serpent's deception, they lost their dominion. The glory was taken from them, and they stood stripped and naked.

But just as the prodigal upon returning to his father's house was given the ring of authority, so, in our restored condition in Christ, we have been made to sit with Him in heavenly places. There, far above all principalities and powers, we are to reign as kings. But we must adhere to God's requirements for kingship if we are to enjoy a blessed, victorious reign.

God's Kingship Requirements

Long before Israel demanded a king, God laid down His requirements for those who would lead His people. Moses was warned by God that certain guidelines were essential in choosing a king (see Deut. 17:14-20). First, the king must be one chosen from among the Israelites' own brethren: He could not be a foreigner. Second, the king was forbidden to acquire great numbers of horses for himself or make the people return to Egypt to get more of them. Third, the king was commanded not to take many wives. Fourth, he was forbidden to accumulate large amounts of silver and gold. And fifth, the king was to write his own personal copy of God's law, read it all the days of his life, and follow it carefully.

As you and I seek to gain insight from God's requirements for kings, we must keep in mind that, though these guidelines no longer apply to us literally, they nonetheless have been "written for our instruction" (Rom. 15:4).

Abhor the Flesh

The first requirement God gave Moses was that no foreigner could be chosen to rule over His people. In the Old Testament, a foreigner was anyone who was uncircumcised.

The rite of circumcision effected admission to the fellowship of God's covenant people and secured to the individual as a member of the nation his share in the promises God made to the nation as a whole. Circumcision reminded the Israelites of God's promises to them and of the duties they had assumed.

While circumcision is physical, its real emphasis is spiritual. The prophets often reminded Israel that the outward rite, to have any significance, must be accompanied by a "circumcision of the heart" (Deut. 30:6; Lev. 26:41). Paul also spoke of the dangers of outward circumcision that was not accompanied by a spiritual change (see Phil. 3:2).

The rite had a moral significance, for we see it metaphorically applied to the *heart* (see Deut. 30:6; Rom. 2:29), the *lips* (see Ex. 6:12,30), and the *ears* (see Jer. 6:10). To meet God's requirement for kingship, believers must not allow the corrupt desires of the flesh to operate (see Col. 2:11-13). The heart, ears, and lips must be sanctified, governed no longer by the flesh, but by the Spirit.

An important principle surfaces when we read the account of God sending Samuel to anoint a king as Saul's replacement. The prophet made a preliminary choice based upon the outward appearance of Jesse's firstborn son. Although Samuel was convinced that Eliab was the right man because of his striking external attributes, God informed the prophet that He had looked at Eliab's heart and rejected him (see 1 Sam. 16:7).

Eliab's heart, the "internal," was not right, and ultimately it was manifested "externally." A short time after Samuel anointed David, Eliab's youngest brother, Eliab's true nature was revealed as he overheard David conversing with Israeli soldiers about Goliath, the Philistine's champion:

> *...And Eliab's anger was aroused against David, and he said, "Why did you come down here? And with whom have you left those few sheep in the wilderness? I know your pride and the insolence of your heart, for you have come down to see the battle"* (1 Samuel 17:28 NJK).

The "internal" determines the "external." Uncircumcised hearts eventually result in unsanctified lives. Little wonder why God commands that those holding positions of leadership be persons of exemplary character and integrity.

Abandon Self-Sufficiency

Not being permitted to acquire great numbers of horses may seem like a strange requirement for kingship until we understand that in Old Testament times, horses stood for power and self-reliance. David said, "Some trust in chariots, and some in horses; but we will remember the name of the Lord our God" (Ps. 20:7).

How easy it becomes for a "king" to trust in his own strength, his own resources. We must rule over our desire for independence, remaining in a position of humility and dependence before God.

God had to severely discipline David for this very reason. After reigning for a time, David decided he would number the people. His motive was not simply to take a census but to determine how many fighting men he had at his disposal.

Although Joab, commander of David's army, attempted to dissuade him, David persisted. The king sought to glory in his own strength, and God judged him for his folly: 70,000 men were slain. The very thing David gloried in was taken from him. As someone has sagely observed, David's sin of passion cost two lives; his sin of pride, 70,000!

If we are to reign as God intended, you and I must recognize the importance of our total dependency upon the Lord. The moment we become self-sufficient, we expose ourselves to manifold problems.

Israel's king was also forbidden to return to Egypt or to send others there for horses. Why? In the Bible, Egypt represents the world, its ways, and our former manner of life. No wonder Isaiah warns us regarding involvement with Egypt:

Woe to those who go down to Egypt for help, and rely on horses, and trust in chariots because they are...very strong, but they do not look to the Holy One of Israel, nor seek the Lord! ...Now the Egyptians are men, and not God, and their horses are flesh and not spirit... (Isaiah 31:1-3).

Egypt typifies man's methods, man's resources, man's wisdom, and his reliance upon the flesh. As persons destined to rule, may you and I abandon all self-sufficiency and learn to rely upon God rather than upon our weak, unreliable flesh or the ways and resources of the world.

Abstain From Sexual Immorality

A third requirement for Israel's king was that he was not to take many wives. As king, he must learn to rule over his passions and desires.

Solomon, David's son, serves as a tragic example of one who presumptuously ignored this command:

> *But King Solomon loved many foreign women...from the nations of whom the Lord had said to the children of Israel, "You shall not intermarry with them, nor they with you. Surely they will turn away your hearts after their gods." Solomon clung to these in love. And he had seven hundred wives, princesses, and three hundred concubines; and his wives turned away his heart. For it was so, when Solomon was old, that his wives turned his heart after other gods; and his heart was not loyal to the Lord his God, as was the heart of his father David. ... Then Solomon built a high place for Chemosh the abomination of Moab, on the hill that is east of Jerusalem, and for Molech the abomination of the people of Ammon. And he did likewise for all his foreign wives, who burned incense and sacrificed to their gods. So the Lord became angry with Solomon, because his heart had turned from the Lord God of Israel, who had appeared to him twice* (1 Kings 11:1-4,7-9 NKJ).

Think of it! Solomon was not some heathen steeped in ignorance and mysticism. He knew God's commands. He *knew* the Lord by intimate, personal acquaintance, for the Lord had appeared to him twice! Yet he presumptuously, flagrantly disobeyed God's direct commands. And that disobedience brought irreparable loss and suffering to his family and the nation he ruled.

How many of God's choicest servants have been destroyed because of their failure in this area? Not possessing the self-control to rule their own spirits, they have allowed themselves the pleasure of sin for a season.

Proverbs warns: "Do not let your heart turn aside to her ways, do not stray into her paths. For many are the victims she has cast down, and numerous are all her slain" (Prov. 7:25-26). And Colossians 3:5 commands: "Put to death, therefore, whatever belongs to your earthly nature: sexual immorality, impurity, lust, evil desires and greed, which is idolatry" (NIV).

The tide of moral failure increases daily. Tragically, Christian superstars are in the lead: television personalities, musicians, authors, and church leaders who seem to think nothing of the examples they are setting. The immediate impact is devastation, and the resulting hurts, bitterness, and confusion may take years to heal.

In striking contrast to these weak-willed, passion-driven leaders, stands the example of Lottie Moon. As a single woman, she overcame great obstacles to bring the gospel to the people of north China. Through Lottie's influence, thousands of missionaries have been sent out and thousands of souls have been brought to faith in Christ.

This lovely woman, with delicate features and beautiful eyes that revealed a will of steel, believed she could be an effective leader, even as an unmarried woman of the nineteenth century. Although Lottie had sisters who were doctors and business executives, Lottie's commitment was to missions. And that commitment came first—even when a boyfriend proposed to her. The young man, a professor, believed in evolution, and Lottie could not endorse his belief. Although she had strong feelings for him, Lottie refused his marriage proposal.

Years later when Lottie was asked about her decision, she replied, "God had first claim on my life, and since the two conflicted, there could be no question about the result."

Lottie established a Chinese church where she saw over a thousand people converted to Christ and baptized. Compassionate, yet tough-minded and courageous, Lottie was not afraid to ruffle some feathers. Chiding Christian men in America for their lack of concern, she wrote, "It is odd that a million Baptists of the South can furnish only three men for all China. ...I wonder how these things look in heaven. They certainly look very strange in China."

After the Boxer Rebellion in China in 1900, Lottie labored tirelessly to minister to victims of the conflict. Smallpox, famine, plagues, and local fighting brought mass starvation to the Tengchow area where Lottie lived. Determined to help her beloved Chinese people, Lottie exhausted her physical strength and drained her life's savings.

Friends, concerned about her weakening health, urged her to return to the States for medical treatment. Lottie died on a ship returning to America on Christmas Eve, 1912.

This courageous woman refused to allow passion and personal concerns to rob her of God's highest and best purpose for her life. Because of her self-control and consecration to God, thousands of souls have entered the Kingdom of God.

If we are to reign victoriously as kings, we must reign over our passions. As Paul reminds us, we must discipline the body and make it our slave, lest after we have preached to others, we ourselves should become disqualified (see 1 Cor. 9:27).

The choice is simple: either we control our desires, or our desires will control us, damaging our effectiveness for God and destroying His highest purposes for our lives.

Avoid the Love of Money

A fourth area over which God required self-restraint by the king involved his personal finances: "...Neither shall he greatly multiply to himself silver and gold'' (Deut. 17:17 KJV). The king was not to be continually scheming and striving to acquire more wealth.

God's Word repeatedly warns us concerning the love of wealth. Consider this sobering injunction from Paul, for example:

*But those who crave to be rich fall into temptation and a snare, and into many foolish (useless, godless) and hurtful desires that plunge men into ruin and **destruction** and miserable perishing. For the love of money is a root of all evils; it is through this craving that some have been led astray, and have wandered from the faith and **pierced** themselves through with many acute [mental] pangs* (1 Timothy 6:9-10 AMP, emphasis mine).

In verse 9, the word *destruction* means to destroy utterly, to perish. The idea is not extinction but ruin and loss of well-being.

In verse 10, the word *pierced* means to put on a spit. Imagine a man, pierced through by a spit, slowly turning over an open fire. This is the sort of soul torture experienced by the insatiably greedy who have strayed from the faith.

No wonder Agur asked God to keep him from riches, lest in his abundance he deny and forget God (see Prov. 30:8-9). In His parable of the seed and the sower, Jesus spoke of unproductive seed that fell among thorns:

And as for what fell among the thorns, these are [the people] who hear, but as they go on their way they are choked and suffocated with the anxieties and cares and riches and pleasures of life, and their fruit does not ripen— come to maturity and perfection (Luke 8:14 AMP).

And who can forget Christ's warning to the rich young ruler? ''How hard it is for those who are wealthy to enter the kingdom of God!'' (Lk. 18:24.)

Unbalanced prosperity teaching fails its hearers in that it presents only one side of the truth. Actually, there is blessed money, and there is cursed money. Money accrued and used with the wrong motives and methods brings a curse upon the greedy, proud, and power-hungry.

When it came to the matter of prosperity, Paul advocated balance and sharing:

Our desire is not that others might be relieved while you are hard pressed, but that there might be equality. At the present time your plenty will supply what they need, so that in turn their plenty will supply what you need. Then there will be equality, as it is written: "He who gathered much did not have too much, and he who gathered little did not have too little" (2 Corinthians 8:13-15 NIV).

Paul then offered this further instruction on finances:

And God is able to make all grace abound to you, so that in all things at all times, having all that you need, you will abound in every good work. As it is written: "He has scattered abroad His gifts to the poor; His righteousness endures forever." Now He who supplies seed to the sower and bread for food will also supply and increase your store of seed and will enlarge the harvest of your righteousness. You will be made rich in every way so that you can be generous on every occasion... (2 Corinthians 9:8-11 NIV).

As one preacher put it, "God doesn't prosper us so we can *drown* in the gravy, but so we can *pass* the gravy."

Because a king is in a position of power, it becomes easy for him to abuse his office and use his position and influence for selfish gain. But sorrow and suffering are the result. Nothing is more tragic than a person possessing power who can't control his own greed.

Adhere to God's Commands

God's fifth and final requirement was that the king thoroughly acquaint himself with God's law and adhere to its commands. He was to write for himself on a scroll a copy of the law. He was to keep that scroll and read it all the days of his life. Why?

> *...So that he may learn to revere the Lord his God and follow carefully all the words of this law and these decrees and not **consider himself better than his brothers** and turn from the law to the right or to the left. Then he and his descendants will reign a long time over his kingdom in Israel* (Deuteronomy 17:19-20 NIV, emphasis mine).

Referring to the Bible, someone once said, "Either this Book will keep you from sin, or sin will keep you from this Book." What an astute observation.

If a king was ignorant of God's commands and principles for living, if he neglected God's Word, it soon became easy to excuse and rationalize away his sins and shortcomings. Before long, he thought nothing of bending and twisting the Scriptures to conform to his own desires rather than conforming himself to the Word's unchanging standards. Eventually, the king would become ensnared in the fatal trap into which so many people of power and position have fallen: that of considering himself "better than his brothers" (Deut. 17:20 NIV)—above the law, exempt from its demands, untouchable.

If we want successful, victorious reigns, we must obey the command God gave His servant Joshua:

This Book of the Law shall not depart from your mouth, but you shall meditate in it day and night, that you may observe to do according to all that is written in it. For then you will make your way prosperous, and then you will have good success (Joshua 1:8 NKJ).

Prosperity. Success. Rich rewards for the believer who meditates daily upon the Word of God and orders each step thereby.

The Key to Reigning in Life

God's standards for kings remain strict. An individual who has not learned self-control will make a weak and dangerous king. If you and I are to be mature believers, people God can trust with kingship, we must abhor the flesh, abandon self-sufficiency, abstain from sexual immorality, avoid the love of money, and adhere to God's commands. As we yield our desires to Christ, His Kingdom is established in our midst, and we reign with Him.

There is no question that God desires His people to reign. We have His promise: "To him who overcomes I will grant to sit with Me on My throne" (Rev. 3:21a NKJ). While this verse is often interpreted prophetically, I believe it also has a present application, for God has "raised us up together, and made us sit together in the heavenly places in Christ Jesus" (Eph. 2:6 NKJ).

We have been raised and seated together with Him. He has given us power and authority. Although these teachings have sometimes been taken to the extreme, their powerful truths have not been invalidated.

God *does* intend for His people to reign in life. The early Church didn't just defend the gospel; they demonstrated it. Through them, God's power was transformed from mere words to mighty acts of healing and deliverance. The powers of hell could not prevail against the force of the gospel they preached. Cities were transformed. The world was turned upside-down for God.

We, too, can move in signs and wonders. We, too, can see lives, churches, cities, and governments transformed. But before God will allow His people to reign externally, He first requires them to rule internally. The internal becomes the key to the external. Christ first seeks to establish His Kingdom *within* us before He can establish His Kingdom *through* us.

King or Slave?

Paul declares that those who receive God's overflowing grace and the free gift of righteousness, putting them into right standing with Himself, will "...reign as kings in life through the One, Jesus Christ..." (Rom. 5:17 AMP).

Then Paul cautions:

> ***Let not sin therefore rule as king*** *in your mortal (short-lived, perishable) bodies, to make you yield to their cravings and be subject to their lusts and evil passions. Do not continue offering or yielding your bodily members [and faculties] to sin as instruments (tools) of wickedness. But offer and yield yourselves to God as though you have been raised from the dead to [perpetual] life, and your bodily members [and faculties] to God, presenting them as implements of righteousness. For sin shall not [any longer] exert dominion over you, since now you are not under Law [as slaves], but under grace—as subjects of God's favor and mercy* (Romans 6:12-14 AMP, emphasis mine).

The choice is clear. We can yield ourselves to God and exert dominion over our sinful flesh and reign as kings in life, or we can yield ourselves to sin, allow sin to rule as king in our bodies, and become its slaves.

King Solomon spoke of a strange paradox. He said, "I have seen servants upon horses, and princes walking as servants upon the earth" (Eccles. 10:7 KJV). Servants riding.... Princes walking as servants.... Are you reigning in life, or have you allowed sin to become your master? Are you riding or walking?

Endnotes

1. The information in this section was taken from Charles L. Mee, Jr., "That Fateful Moment When Two Civilizations Came Face to Face," *Smithsonian* (Vol. 23, No. 7, October 1992), pp. 57-69.

Chapter Eleven

Instructions for Believers as Priests

As we have seen, God intended mankind from the beginning to have a twofold function—that of king and priest. The function of the king was to be governmental. The function of the priest was sacrificial and mediatorial.

Israel, after having been delivered from Egypt, cried out to Moses: "Why, now, have you brought us up from Egypt...?" (Ex. 17:3) God responded by telling Moses: "Thus you shall say of the house of Jacob and tell the sons of Israel...'You shall be to Me a kingdom of priests and a holy nation' " (Ex. 19:3).

As you know, the Old Testament is very much an illustration book of spiritual principles. What we see there transpiring in the natural often has its counterpart in the spiritual realm. God frequently uses Old Testament types and symbols to convey spiritual truth to His Church today. As a matter of fact, Romans 15:4 tells us what was written in former days was written for our instruction. We see this fact illustrated in the Book of Leviticus, where God sets forth certain requirements for those ministering as His priests.

Requirements for Spiritual Service

Not only were priests required to belong to the tribe of Levi, but certain physical requirements were also demanded of them. For example, they could not be blind or lame. (See Leviticus 21:17-20.)

But if man looks on the outward appearance and God looks on the heart (see 1 Sam. 16:7), why did God require physical perfection for spiritual service? The answer can be found only in viewing the physical as an illustration or object lesson of the spiritual requirements God expects in His people, especially in His leaders or those aspiring to leadership.

In Old Testament times, every son of Aaron was a priest. His priestly status resulted from being a descendant of Aaron, Israel's high priest, just as every Christian becomes a priest unto God when we are born into His family through our union with Christ, our great high priest.

Any son of Aaron who had a defect or blemish was disqualified from certain priestly functions. Though these physical requirements for spiritual service are no longer in effect, it is important we don't bypass the lessons they teach. Just as God set forth certain requirements for eldership in the New Testament, providing a standard to which others should aspire whether or not they are elders, likewise through the requirements for priestly ministering, God reveals the standards He desires for us.

Leviticus 21 lists 11 defects that disqualified sons of Aaron from performing some of the higher ministries of priestly service and worship:

And the Lord spoke to Moses, saying, "Speak to Aaron, saying: 'No man of your descendants in succeeding generations, who has any defect, may approach to offer the bread of his God. For any man who has a defect shall not approach: a man blind or lame, who has a marred face or any limb too long, a man who has a broken foot or broken hand, or is a hunchback or a dwarf, or a man who has a defect in his eye, or eczema or scab, or is a eunuch. No man of the descendants of Aaron the priest, who has a defect, shall come near to offer the offerings made by fire to the Lord. He has a defect; he shall not come near to offer the bread of his God. He may eat the bread of his God, both the most holy and the holy; only he shall not go near the veil or approach the altar, because he has a defect, lest he profane My sanctuaries; for I the Lord sanctify them'" (Leviticus 21:16-23 NKJ).

Although you and I are priests unto God by virtue of our living relationship with Christ, our privileges as priests are dependent and conditional. Like the sons of Aaron, we can be excluded from higher, honored ministries for the Lord. Let's examine each disqualification listed in Leviticus 21 and consider the spiritual significance for believers today.

Blindness: Lack of Revelation

A son of Aaron who was blind could not perform certain priestly duties. Although this prerequisite deals with physical blindness, it is interesting to note that the Bible speaks far more often about spiritual blindness.

The Bible declares that there are things that eye has not seen and ear has not heard, but that God has revealed to us "through His Spirit" (1 Cor. 2:9-10). One of the essential requirements for our priestly calling is that we have a clear perception of spiritual matters.

We see this important principle demonstrated in Paul's prayers that believers would be given a spirit of wisdom and revelation in the knowledge of God and that the eyes of their heart might be enlightened so they might know the hope of God's calling (see Eph. 1:17-18). We're also reminded of this vital principal by David's prayer, "Open my eyes, that I may behold wonderful things from Thy law" (Ps. 119:18).

For many, the Word of God is a closed book, a dry, historical record of events having little or no personal significance. It is as if a veil remains over their minds, a veil only the Spirit of God can lift. Because the minds and spiritual eyes of the Pharisees were clouded by such a veil, Jesus accused the Pharisees of being "blind leaders of the blind." Not seeing where they themselves were going, the Pharisees were unable to lead others.

One of the reasons for which Jesus received His anointing was to bring sight to the blind, both physically and spiritually. Like the disciples on the road to Emmaus, how desperately we need the Lord to open our eyes and minds that we might behold Him afresh and understand the Scriptures. Then we can serve Him more acceptably as New Testament priests.

Lameness: Lack of Consistency

A lame man could not qualify for certain priestly functions in Moses' day. What significance does this hold for you and me?

The word for *lame* means to hop, hesitate, or limp. This is the individual who is inconsistent, whose spiritual life isn't steady and predictable, but tends to fluctuate easily.

During the reign of Ahab, Elijah the prophet challenged idolatrous Israel with these words: "...How long halt ye between two opinions? If the Lord be God, follow Him: but if Baal, then follow him..." (1 Kings 18:21 KJV). This Hebrew word translated *halt* is the identical word translated *lame*. Israel as a nation was vacillating between God and Baal. Elijah, tired of their inconsistency, drew a line and demanded that Israel choose one side or the other. No more wavering. No more fluctuating. No more going back and forth.

Likewise, the New Testament priest must be consistent and steadfast, not swayed by circumstances or feelings. We are to walk "even as He walked."

Disfigured Face: Lack of Discrimination

A son of Aaron could be disqualified because his face was marred by a permanent defect such as a badly broken nose. You see, long before the eyes can detect certain problems, the nose can discern that something is wrong. Since one of the major functions of the priest was to instruct the people to discern between the unclean and the clean (see Ezek. 44:23), he needed a keen sense of smell.

For any man who has a blemish, he shall not approach a lame man or a blind man or one whose nose is cut off... (Leviticus 21:18, Lamsa Translation).

A friend once told me how he awoke one night with a burning smell in his nostrils. Within minutes, his house was destroyed by fire, but he managed to save his family. In summing up his story, my friend said, "My nose saved me."

There has never been a time like today when we so desperately need the ability to discern. The Bible tells us to examine everything carefully and hold fast to that which is good, and, as spiritual people, to judge all things. Things may appear to be fine, as when the Gibeonites deceived Joshua (see Josh. 9:3-14) or when Jacob deceived his father (see Gen. 27). Jesus clearly taught that deception will be one of the major problems we face in the last days. False Christs, false teachers, and false prophets will arise, and with signs and wonders will seek to deceive even the elect (see Mt. 24:24).

Only as we begin to call upon the Lord for discernment can we be saved from the deceptive tactics of the enemy. Our only hope is to cry out for discernment and lift our voice for understanding; then we will discern—and discover the knowledge of God (see Prov. 2:3-5).

Deformed Limb: Lack of Proportion

A casual glance at a believer's bookcase will often provide a good indication of the spiritual food he ingests. Most of us are inclined to gravitate to what we like rather than to what we need. Like the youngster who would rather have ice cream than spinach, we often suffer from an unbalanced spiritual diet. Many Christians suffer from an overemphasis on one aspect of truth to the detriment of another. How easy it becomes to major on extremes: law vs. grace, faith vs. works, gifts vs. fruit, God's sovereignty vs. our free will, etc., instead of rightly dividing the Word of truth.

Take, for example, the life of Christ. We can divide His life into three categories: His person, purpose, and power. Some churches major on the person of Christ, and their teaching revolves around His character. The emphasis is on themes such as righteousness and holiness. Other churches emphasize His purpose, stressing the value of evangelism and missions. Saving the lost becomes a supreme objective. Meanwhile, the power of God is emphasized by those who see the need for miracles and healings, and their diet becomes solely the supernatural. Nothing is wrong with any of these views. The Scriptures abound with support for each of them. But to emphasize one at the expense of another causes an imbalance—believers grow up with improper proportions.

The Word teaches that we are to grow up in all aspects like unto Him (see Eph. 4:15). We are to be complete in Christ (see Col. 2:10). Are you balanced? Are certain aspects of your spiritual life out of proportion?

Broken Foot: Lack of Dominion

God's intention has always been for man to have dominion. Throughout the Scriptures, the foot is always used in conjunction with dominion. From Genesis, where God told man to "subdue," which means literally "to tread down," through Revelation, man was to rule.

The Scriptures are replete with examples of this fundamental principle. Israel was promised by God that every place their feet would tread, God would give it to them. Jesus, who has all things in subjection under His feet (see Eph. 1:22), told His disciples that He was giving them the authority to tread upon serpents and scorpions and over all the power of the enemy (see Lk. 10:19).

Why do so many believers today suffer from defeat and discouragement? Surely they have never known how to overcome and take the victory. As New Testament priests, we need to understand the authority we have in Christ.

Broken Hand: Lack of Impartation

Laying on of hands occurs throughout the Word. Repeatedly, when hands were laid on someone, there was an "impartation." Jesus often laid hands upon people for healing or blessing, as in the case of little children. Hands were laid on those separated by the Holy Ghost for ministry. Through the laying on of hands, people received the filling of the Holy Spirit and also gifts of the Spirit. Wisdom was given to Joshua when Moses laid his hand upon him.

God has called us to be imparters of life. Broken-handed people are unable to minister to others; instead, they need others to minister to them. You and I must be able to say with Jesus, "I came not to be ministered unto, but to minister..." (see Mt. 20:28).

Hunchback: Lack of Liberation

As a child in my father's church, I remember one member of the congregation, an older woman, who was terribly hunchbacked. So bad was her condition that she couldn't look up; her head was forever down.

Similarly, in the Christian life, some believers are spiritual "hunchbacks," bound by their failures and insecurities. Constantly looking down and within, they have never known the liberty Christ can bring. How we need to be like the Psalmist who rejoiced that the Lord was his glory and the lifter of his head.

Luke tells of the woman who for 18 years was doubled over, unable to straighten up. The woman was a true daughter of Abraham, who faithfully attended God's house, yet she was bound. Luke relates what happened when this dear, hunchbacked woman encountered the healing Christ:

> But when Jesus saw her, He called her to Him and said to her, "Woman, you are loosed from your infirmity." And He laid His hands on her, and immediately she was made straight, and glorified God (Luke 13:12-13 NKJ).

Are there areas of your life that need to be made straight? Bring them to Jesus. His truth and healing power will set you free.

Dwarf: Lack of Maturation

The dwarf represents the believer who has never reached his full potential in Christ. Not having attained unto full stature, he remains a babe.

Paul describes this dwarfed, immature condition when addressing the Corinthians. He reminds them that he can only feed them milk, not meat. The writer to the Hebrews also admonishes the immature that they have had time to grow and should be teachers, yet they still have need of being taught.

Why is it that some believers never grow up? Some are satisfied to remain as babies. Others, because of lack of teaching, are ignorant of God's intention for them. And many, having no root in themselves because of the thin, rocky soil of their hearts, depend upon others to meet their needs and solve their problems when affliction, trouble, or persecution comes (see Mt. 13:20-21).

The Christian life is always progressive. We are to move from faith to faith, from victory to victory, ever increasing and abounding in the knowledge of Christ. If you've stopped growing, you simply need to start again. Press on to maturity. Nourish your spirit on His Word each day. This requires a sincere desire and determined effort to study the Word and walk in obedience to it, but a spiritual growth spurt will be the rewarding result.

Defective Eyes: Lack of Clarification

The defective eye typifies the believer who lacks a sense of clear vision and understanding. Unlike the blind who have no light whatsoever, there are those who, though having light, can't focus properly or see clearly. Like the blind man for whom Jesus prayed, they see only "men as trees, walking." But when Jesus touched him a second time, he saw everything clearly (see Mk. 8:22-25).

Many Christians are nearsighted, unable to see at a distance. They have little long-range vision. Others are farsighted, unable to see things close up. Both problems present difficulties in the spiritual sense.

The shortsighted person is so taken up with the present, he becomes bogged down with his circumstances and trials. He is not able to see what God can produce through him for the future.

The farsighted, on the other hand, never comes to terms with the present. He lives in the unreality of the future. As Proverbs 17:24 says, "...The eyes of a fool are on the ends of the earth."

God has only one standard for His people: perfection. In His love and patience, God accepts us as we are, but He continually holds before us the ideal of what He designed us to become. Therefore, we must keep "looking unto Jesus the author and finisher of our faith..." (Heb. 12:2).

Eczema, Scabs: Lack of Purification

Throughout the Scriptures, various skin conditions are used to typify sin, rebellion, and evil. Leprosy, for example, invariably is linked with rebellion in the Scriptures. And one of the penalties God gave to Israel for disobedience was that He would curse them with "boils, scabs, and itch." The nation's sinful internal condition was manifested externally. We see this principle illustrated when Isaiah, describing Israel's sinful condition, likens her to a body covered in sores from head to toe.

Sin in the life of a priest, a spiritual leader, would be especially tragic, for a sinful example, like certain skin diseases, can be contagious. The priest, as God's representative, was to live an exemplary life, above reproach.

Christ is returning for a Church without spot, wrinkle, or any such thing. Oh, how we need a new move of holiness and purity, for the priests "shall be holy...and not profane the name of their God..." (Lev. 21:6 KJV).

Crushed Stones: Lack of Reproduction

There was no worse stigma in Old Testament times than barrenness, the inability to reproduce. Proverbs says there are three things that can't be satisfied, and one is the barren womb.

One of God's desires for His children is that we experience the joy of leading others to Christ and seeing Christ formed in them. God's Word promises: "Those who are wise shall shine like the brightness of the firmament, and those who turn many to righteousness like the stars forever and ever" (Dan. 12:3 NKJ). What is your condition? Fruitful or barren?

Priests Unto God

We need to understand that God requires certain qualities in those He chooses for service. Although we New Testament priests live in another dispensation, God still demands that His people be adequate, furnished, and equipped for every good work (see 2 Tim. 3:17).

We are all unclean from our continual defilement with the "dead," contaminating things of earth, but "our life is hid with Christ in God," and because of our living relationship with Him, we remain priests. Yet we continue to battle the defects that would disqualify us from serving His highest and holiest purposes for us: weakness of disposition, infirmities in character, vacillation in will and purpose, moral impurity, spiritual shortsightedness, deformed spirits, imperfections of heart, and so forth.

We must not assume that all Christians enjoy the identical intimacy of fellowship or the same nearness of Christ. All believers enjoy sonship, but our defects relegate us to varying levels of service and can deprive us of many high and holy privileges.

If we are to occupy posts of dignity and move in the public gaze, God's standards demand the most noble qualities of character. But even the lowliest, least public ministries are sacred to God. If we are to have power with Him and enjoy His overflowing presence, we must be consistent in our private conduct. We must separate ourselves from all that is forbidden and consecrate ourselves to all that is commanded.

The ancient priest was required to be physically perfect, for he represented the perfect humanity found in Israel's Priest Messiah. As New Testament priests, you and I represent Him who is "altogether lovely," the perfect Priest, our Lord Jesus Christ. May we strive to be conformed to Him in every way.

Section Three

Fulfilling the Vision

Chapter Twelve

Your Ministry of Intercession

Ministry is a natural by-product of maturity. Not every believer is called to be a pastor, teacher, evangelist, prophet, or apostle, but everyone in the body of Christ is called to minister.

The ministry of the Old Testament priest was one of sacrifice and service. Of course, it's no longer our responsibility to offer up literal sacrifices, for Christ became the ultimate sacrifice for sin. But as priests under the New Covenant, you and I are to offer up spiritual sacrifices to God through Christ (see 1 Pet. 2:5).

I believe the New Testament assigns us three definite ministries: intercession, celebration, and proclamation. First, let's focus on our priestly ministry of intercession.

Intercessory Prayer

What is intercessory prayer, anyway? I like what Richard J. Foster, author of *Prayer: Finding the Heart's True Home*, says:

"If we truly love people, we will desire for them far more than it is within our power to give them, and this will lead us to prayer. Intercession is a way of loving others.

"When we move from petition to intercession we are shifting our center of gravity from our own needs to the needs and concerns of others. Intercessory prayer is selfless prayer, even self-giving prayer.

"In the ongoing work of the kingdom of God, nothing is more important than intercessory prayer. People today desperately need the help that we can give them. Marriages are being shattered. Children are being destroyed. Individuals are living lives of quiet desperation, without purpose or future. And we can make a difference...if we will learn to pray on their behalf.

"...As priests, appointed and anointed by God, we have the honor of going before the Most High on behalf of others. This is not optional; it is a sacred obligation—and a precious privilege—of all who take up the yoke of Christ."[1]

Every time the Old Testament high priest entered the tabernacle, he bore before the Lord the names of the 12 tribes. He represented them before God, pleading on their behalf.

Likewise, Jesus as our High Priest "ever liveth to make intercession for [us]" (Heb. 7:25 KJV). Our prayers are undergirded and reinforced by the prayers of our eternal Intercessor.

Paul exhorts Timothy that intercessions be made for all men, not only for our own sake (that we may lead a quiet and peaceable life), but also because God desires all men to be saved and come to the knowledge of the truth (see 1 Tim. 2:1-4). One wonders what the condition of the world would be like today if the Church had faithfully maintained those principles.

Nations can be born in a day, but only as Zion travails does she bring forth. You and I have been challenged to ask God for the nations as our inheritance and the uttermost parts of the earth as our possession, but it is through prayer and praise that we bind kings and nobles with fetters of iron and execute vengeance on the nations (see Ps. 2:8-10).

Prayer makes the most unlikely thing a possibility and the unexpected a glorious surprise. Intercession knows no boundaries; no limitations are placed in its path. No wonder, then, that the enemy labors to blind our understanding concerning prayer.

For the average believer, prayer is merely a required formality, a means whereby he relieves guilt and measures spirituality. Where are the true intercessors who are willing to hold onto God until nations are visited from on high, until those blinded by satanic deception are made to see, until those held in prisons of religious bondage are set free by Christ?

Putting the Impossible in Our Range

Prayer originates in God. It is the activity of His nature to lay hold of the implications of the cross and administer them. We have been called to sit with Christ in heavenly places, far above all rule and authority. To us has been given the "key" to unlocking the power of God. By His cross, Christ arrested and abolished our impotence and paralysis, and by "a new and living way" created an eternal highway into His omnipotence and dominion. (See Hebrews 10:19-22 and Ephesians 2:18.)

Here is the sphere that the cross has now thrown open to all who will come to it. Here we surmount the problems of distance and space, ignorance and opposition, frustration and perplexity, and any other obstacle one cares to name. All are conquered by Christ through His cross. In union with Him, the "impossible" is our range, as well as His. Where He goes, we can go. What He does, we can do. Moreover, all God's promises have to be mediated in Christ through us (see 2 Cor. 1:20). Not through angels, but through us—the redeemed!

What a gospel! What a life! What a calling! The Christian life has nothing to do with the possible, but the impossible. It is another sphere, another order, another law. For the one who prays, the cross has not only opened free access to God but has also inspired contact with man. Through Christ there is a blood-stained track for us to the heart of men everywhere. If we act on these truths in faith, we can traverse continents, invade nations, and make history by manifesting the program of God. That is the business of faith, and it functions through prayer. If not, the disciples could never have prayed, "Thy kingdom come. Thy will be done on earth."

In prayer, distance is nothing. It "gets there" faster than the speed of sound. Yet, it's more wonderful than that. God liquidates common sense, silences reasoning, rules out logic, and demonstrates His almighty power by making the miraculous an everyday affair. How else can we interpret Isaiah 65:24, where God says, "Before [you] call, I will answer" (KJV). What a blessing that He anticipates not only our needs, but our prayers.

Praying people can tell you of answers that must have been on the way before they put their requests into words. This is the natural result of union with Christ and cooperation with God. This is the big business of being linked with God in His universal purposes—what Paul describes as being "called into the fellowship of God's Son." That's God's will, Christianity in action!

Christ died that whosoever—everyone, everywhere, all the time—might come to Him. Think, then, what a vast field of activity is open to the believer. Want to be used? Here's your chance. Want a sense of accomplishment? Nothing produces it so adequately as praying. Pray out of living union with Christ. Challenge the wreck and ruin of the Fall. Claim the enforcement of God's eternal purpose on His cross, and embrace the universe!

Recognizing the Enemy's Tactics

The enemy is ever mindful of the fact that if we ever arise to our calling as priests, his purposes will be severely hindered. So for this reason, he seeks to blind us to our full potential. Using the many tools at his disposal—doubt, fear, failure, and ignorance—he seeks to dissuade us from moving from mere knowledge to the application of it.

Sending Doubts and Discouragement

Perhaps you pray consistently for a time because you feel like praying. Then something happens to rob you of the desire. Discouragement sets in. Maybe you stumble in some other area of your walk with God. If you are not properly anchored in Christ, the accuser will point his finger at you. He'll attempt to muzzle and paralyze you, and with all the attendant miseries and calamities, you will feel inclined to stop praying. Have none of that!

It is a ghastly mistake to suppose that we have no right to pray because we have slipped up. But because we so easily believe that, we become either absent or dumb at prayer time. The devil laughs, because he has succeeded for a time in robbing us of the opportunity to use our redemptive powers to release his captives, overthrow his government, and enforce his doom.

So settle it once and for all. No matter what you feel like, there is only one basis upon which you can gain and sustain access to God—the finished work of Christ.

"Through Him," writes Paul in Ephesians 2:18, "we...have access by one Spirit unto the Father" (KJV). Access to God! Dare to believe that you can always have access to the heart of God so that at any moment in all circumstances you can have immediate, personal access to your Father, and through Him to the world!

Destroying Our Weapons

During the reign of Saul, the Philistines cunningly destroyed all the blacksmiths in Israel. Why? Because a weaponless army is a powerless army. Without being aware of it, Israel was gradually becoming defenseless, for the blacksmiths were responsible for forging the weapons of war. It was their task to supply the nations with swords, spears, and shields. When the day of battle eventually came, a powerless Israel was defeated (see 1 Sam. 13:19-22).

The enemy's strategy remains the same today. He knows that the prayer meeting is the blacksmith's shop of the Church. Aware of the fact that by prayer the sword of the Spirit can be wielded and battles won, the enemy ever works to destroy prayer, both individually and corporately, from the Church. Normally, the process begins long before the day of battle. Most of us, caught by surprise, are defenseless at the time of our greatest need.

Binding Spiritual Forces

Spiritual warfare is always associated with prayer. One of the major needs of the Church today is for effective "warriors of war"—those prepared to tackle the spiritual forces arrayed against the advancement of God's Kingdom. Jesus stated that unless we first bind the strongman, we can't spoil his goods (see Mt. 12:29). *By "strongman" we mean the spiritual leader in charge of resisting the cause of God, whether it's an individual, a group, a city, or a nation.* This theme becomes more evident as we trace it through the Scriptures.

When Jesus addressed the spirit within the Gadarene demoniac by asking his name, the response came, "My name [singular] is Legion; for we [plural] are many" (Mk. 5:9b NKJ). Here we are told of a "strongman" with numerous other spirits of a lesser rank under him. Understanding the principle of first binding the strongman, Jesus commanded "Legion" to go (verse 8), and soon they all left (verse 13).

Similarly, when Paul was asked to speak to Sergus Paulus, the proconsul, he was resisted by Elymas the magician. Realizing that he was dealing with something beyond human strength, Paul turned to Elymas and took authority over the situation, calling him a "son of the devil" and an "enemy of all righteousness." Immediately the proconsul believed when he saw what happened (see Acts 13:6-12).

Having seen the way the enemy can control an individual, now see what can happen to a city and a nation.

While in Ephesus, Paul encountered some of his greatest opposition. Writing to the Corinthians, he told them of his open door in Ephesus, but added that there were many adversaries.

While Paul was ministering in Ephesus, the entire city was stirred up against him. The riot lasted for hours until finally the town clerk stood and silenced the crowd by reminding them that Ephesus was the stronghold of Diana, the goddess whom the Ephesians believed had come down out of Heaven and established her headquarters among them. As a result, people had come from all over the world to worship in the temple erected to her.

No wonder that, after establishing a church there, Paul wrote to the Ephesians stressing that they were not merely fighting flesh and blood, but principalities and powers (see Eph. 6:12; Acts 19).

A "principality" is an area controlled by a "prince." For example, Wales, which makes up a part of the United Kingdom of Great Britain, is known as the Principality of Wales. The prince over Wales is Prince Charles. Just as we have natural authorities over certain areas, satan has positioned spiritual authorities over certain areas. Satan's kingdom is well organized. It would appear from Scripture that the city of Ephesus was under a satanic prince who was working through the influence of "Diana." We also know from Scripture that entire nations, as well as cities, can be controlled by demonic princes.

Recognizing Two Kingdoms in Conflict

In First Samuel 17, we see the nation of Israel being confronted with Goliath, the Philistine captain, who is a type of the spiritual "strongman." In this story, both nations are standing on mountains, which in Scripture often symbolizes authority, power, or influence. We could liken this to a battle between the Kingdom of God (Israel) and the kingdom of satan (the Philistines).

We understand from the Word that both kingdoms are determined to destroy one another. Jesus came to destroy the works of the devil, whose kingdom is depleted every time someone is born again. Likewise, satan seeks to undermine the effectiveness of God's Kingdom by taking away the seed of the Word of God, when it is sown, by causing people to be blinded by the cares of this life, so as not to produce the fruit of the Kingdom, etc.

Returning to our story, we see Goliath issuing a challenge to Israel asking for an opponent (see 1 Sam. 17:8-10). Goliath is called the *champion*—which literally means "a man with intervention"—one willing to fight for a cause and, if necessary, lay down his life. Goliath is the satanic counterpart to the Christian intercessor who intercedes on behalf of an individual or nation.

The name *Goliath* means "soothsayer." In fact, the Philistines as a people are referred to as being soothsayers (see Is. 2:6)—those being involved in the satanic realm who attempt illegitimately to find out the purposes of God and thwart them, or to substitute the power of evil spirits for the authority of the Word of God.

Goliath, in his challenge to Israel, says that whoever can destroy him [singular] will have all the Philistines [plural] as his servants. Here then is the principle of the strongman: "Bind me, and we will become your servants."

When the Israelites heard the challenge, they were afraid—Saul included. Goliath's challenge continued for 40 days, with no response from Israel until young David arrived in the camp. Suddenly Goliath appeared and issued his challenge again. The moment David saw the situation, I believe, he realized the key to everything lay in destroying Goliath, in binding the strongman. David saw Goliath merely as an uncircumcised Philistine. In comparison, he viewed Israel as "the army of the living God."

It's important that we see ourselves for who we really are—linked to the Almighty, part of God's Army. This is not seeing "our" potential, but what we are "in Christ." Too many Christians see themselves as weak, helpless, struggling children of God. But the Word exhorts us to be "strong in the Lord, and in the strength of His might" (see Eph. 6:10). It's not what we are, but what we can become through Christ who strengthens us. This is what we are to focus upon—not our own weakness.

Saul learned of David's desire to fight Goliath and sent for him but, upon seeing his size, Saul told David that he, a youth, wouldn't stand a chance against Goliath with all his experience. Refusing to back down, David explained his past victories against the lion and bear, telling how God brought deliverance through him.

Perhaps realizing this might be his last chance to assist David, Saul suggested that David use his armor. David, certain the victory would not be won with man's strength, refused.

How often do we seek to go to battle equipped in "Saul's armor"? The Bible says the weapons of our warfare are not "carnal" but mighty through God to the pulling down of strongholds (see 2 Cor. 10:4).

Attacking the Proper Target

As David prepared to fight, he took five stones from the brook and proceeded toward Goliath. Notice that although Goliath was protected by his shield-bearer, David never sought to destroy the shield-bearer: his objective was Goliath.

So often in prayer, we spend far too much time fighting shield-bearers and too little time on the Goliaths. Surely, this is one of satan's great tactics—the use of decoys to drag us away from the real issues. Paul reminds us that our battle is not against flesh and blood, but principalities and powers.

David never wavered in his determination to destroy the "strongman." Approaching the strongman, he revealed the source of his strength: "...I come to you in the name of the Lord of hosts..." (1 Sam. 17:45). David understood what it means to "be strong in the Lord, and in the strength of His might." Not relying upon his own ability, David toppled Goliath with his sling. Then, seizing Goliath's own sword, David cut off his head. As the Philistine army fled in fear, Israel pursued and plundered their goods.

God is looking for believers today who know how to wage effective warfare against the spiritual forces opposing God's Kingdom. Only as we allow the Holy Spirit to open our eyes in the spiritual realm can we see who our real adversaries are. Many organizations are pouring millions of dollars into fighting abortion, humanism, pornography, and various political causes. While these things are wicked and hated by God, the real key lies not in wrestling against flesh and blood, but in binding and defeating the spiritual forces behind those visible problems.

In Exodus 17, God used another battle, this time between Israel and the Amalekites, to underline the importance of the unseen forces in the spiritual realm. When Israel was attacked by the Amalekites, Joshua was told by Moses to choose some men to fight against them. Meanwhile, Moses ascended the mountain to pray. As long as Moses' hands were raised toward God's throne, Israel was victorious. But if Moses dropped his hands in weariness, the Amalekites prevailed. Only when Aaron and Hur supported Moses by lifting his hands did Joshua defeat the Amalekites.

It's important that we have groups prepared to fight in the valley. But far more important is that we have ones behind the scenes who, seated with Christ in the heavenlies, make the difference between victory or defeat.

The Most Significant Job in the Universe

The prayer warrior has the most significant job in the universe. He can marshall the hosts of God wherever they're needed. He can penetrate the secret sessions of satanic schemers, confound their plans, and claim the death sentence of the cross upon all godless government.

If you have never started to move behind the iron curtains of government and satanic conspiracy, do it. If you have never embraced hemispheres and nations in prayer, do it. If you have never invaded the heart of the enemy camp, do it. Say, "Lord, I want to be a faithful priest, standing between God and man, interceding and offering up spiritual sacrifices. I want to be a worker with You in Your universe. Help me to grasp the eternal and embrace the exploits of Your Kingdom."

Endnotes

1. Richard J. Foster, *Prayer: Finding the Heart's True Home* (New York, NY: HarperCollins Pub., 1992), p. 191.

Chapter Thirteen

Celebration
and Proclamation

Intercession is one of our primary functions as New Testament priests. But we must also understand and embrace two other important priestly ministries: celebration and proclamation.

The Ministry of Celebration

All over the world, churches are flowing in a new release of praise and worship to God. Old forms are giving way to new expressions of celebration. Joy is once again returning to the house of the Lord. Books and seminars abound, teaching various methods of worshiping God afresh.

Scripture declares that we, as living stones, are being built together into a spiritual house and that, as a holy priesthood, we are to offer up spiritual sacrifices acceptable to God through Jesus Christ (see 1 Pet. 2:5). Likewise, we're told to continually offer up a sacrifice of praise to God, that is, the fruit of our lips that gives thanks to His name (see Heb. 13:15).

Some teach that the sacrifice of praise is giving God His due, regardless of how we feel. They use "sacrifice" in the sense of "costing" us something. While that may be true, I believe the Scriptures clearly teach that sacrifice speaks of the very best we have to offer, for it was the priests' duty to examine the sacrifices, and only those meeting God's requirements were acceptable.

Ministry or "Magic"?

Today's Church has, in some circles, become obsessed with pageantry, dance, and drama. I wonder how much of this current emphasis on praise and worship is acceptable to God. Much, I fear, is merely outward rather than from the overflow of hearts full of adoration and love.

John Henry Jowett in his devotional *A Daily Meditation* warns against "religion as mere magic." Says Jowett:

> "And when the ark of the covenant of the Lord came into the camp, all Israel shouted with a great shout" (1 Sam. 4:1-11). They were making more of the ark than of the Lord. Their religion was degenerating into superstition. I become superstitious whenever the means of worship are permitted to eclipse the Object of worship. I then possess a magic instrument and I forget the holy Lord. ...So let mine eyes be ever unto the Lord! Let me not be satisfied with the ark, but let me seek Him whose name is holy and whose nature is love."[1]

As Jowett warns, so often the *means* of worship becomes the *object* of worship. We need to ask God for sensitivity to His mind. There are times when I feel the most appropriate thing to do would be to "close the gates"—recognizing that our worship is not acceptable because of our apathy, pride, insincerity, or spiritual ritualism. In such cases, our time would be better spent in humbling ourselves and asking God to "renew a right spirit within us."

It's important to compare our lifestyle with our lips. Only when the two agree is our praise acceptable. Surely the fruit of our lips refers to more than merely our words. Fruit is the outward expression of the inner life. Jesus said of the Pharisees that they honored Him with their lips, but their hearts were far from Him.

Only out of the abundance of the heart can our praise be acceptable to God. Stunning choreography, perfect pitch, and musical skills are far from essential. Clean hands and pure hearts are the ingredients to acceptable worship. The Psalmist says, "Worship the Lord in the beauty of holiness" (Ps. 29:2b KJV). Only when the Lord says, "righteousness and praise spring up before all nations" (see Is. 61:11) will He be satisfied with our "celebration."

The Ministry of Proclamation

As priests, we are also called to "proclamation." Ours is the privilege of proclaiming the gospel. "God chose us as His own possession that we might proclaim His excellencies" (1 Pet. 2:9). We need to understand that proclamation is not reserved for the professional clergy alone, but for every member of the body of Christ. We have too long majored on "celebration," to the detriment of our other responsibilities. But the more involved we become in "intercession" and "proclamation," the greater will be our "celebration."

When Peter and John proclaimed Christ's Lordship to the beggar at the Temple and he was healed, the beggar entered the Temple with them, celebrating—"walking and leaping and praising God." After leaving the Temple, the people saw the miraculous way this man had been healed and they, too, "were all glorifying God for what had happened" (see Acts 3).

In the fifth chapter of Revelation, we see men redeemed from every tribe, tongue, and nation, gathered around the throne.

There, along with the angelic host, they are worshiping the Lamb. How did they arrive at this wonderful time of celebration? They responded to the gospel as it was proclaimed by God's servants performing their priestly service. Without proclamation, there is no celebration.

Let's not shun our responsibility to evangelize. We have no reason to be ashamed of the gospel, for it is the power of God unto salvation. May God grant us a greater measure of boldness to witness for Him. May we ever keep before us the challenge that "this gospel of the kingdom shall be proclaimed in all the world for a witness unto all nations; and then shall the end come" (see Mt. 24:14).

Embracing Our Priestly Ministry

Beginning with the parts rather than the whole leads to error. To major on "intercession" without "celebration" is wrong. But majoring on "celebration" without "proclamation" is also insufficient.

Jesus said, "...Thou shalt worship the Lord thy God, and Him only shalt thou serve" (Lk. 4:8 KJV). Notice that worship devoid of service is an imbalance. Likewise, service without worship is equally unbalanced. The priestly function is three-fold: intercession, celebration, and proclamation. Each is a necessary part of the whole. We must flow in all three if our priestly ministry is to be complete.

Endnotes

1. John Henry Jowett, "Religion as Mere Magic," April 14, in *A Daily Meditation* (La Verne, CA: El Camino Press, n.d.), p. 108.

Chapter Fourteen

Time to Grow Up!

In her book *Blow Away the Black Clouds*, Florence Littauer shares her heartbreaking story of what it is like to give birth to two brain-damaged sons.

Florence and her husband, Fred, already had two little girls when she gave birth to her husband's namesake, Frederick Jerome Littauer III. Life was complete. She was happy. Then the nightmare began.

> "By the time young Frederick III was eight months old, he began to scream fitfully in the night and no longer sat up. His eyes became glassy and he stopped smiling. When these symptoms increased, I took him to my pediatrician, who examined him and called in a specialist. I shall never forget his words: 'This child is hopelessly brain-damaged. You might as well put him away, forget him, and have another one.' "[1]

The word *hopeless* had never been in Florence's vocabulary. Refusing to accept defeat, she and her husband took the baby to the Yale-New Haven Hospital for tests. There they received the same verdict: "He's hopeless."

That memory is still fresh in Florence's memory:

"Then I remembered the doctor's words, 'You might as well put him away, forget him, and have another one.' I couldn't put him away or forget him, but I could have another one. It seemed my only hope. During the nine-month wait for my fourth child, I began to reevaluate my life. I realized I had put my faith in me. In my own power to achieve...

"Yet when I held my dying child, none of these achievements mattered. As I held Freddie tightly through his ten to twelve convulsions a day, as I cried with his screams of pain in the night, my only hope was that my next child would be normal and I could put this nightmare behind me.

"While I was in the hospital giving birth to our second son, Laurence Chapman Littauer, my husband put Freddie in a private children's hospital, where at age two he died of pneumonia.

"With the birth of my second son I became a devoted, almost fanatical mother. I allowed no one to touch Larry but me. I watched him all day and jumped when he cried at night. I gave up all my positions and presidencies—my hope was in Larry. However, one week after Freddie died, I went in to get Larry from his nap, but he didn't respond to my greeting. I picked him up quickly and shook him, crying, 'Smile, Larry, smile!' But Larry didn't smile. I feared the worst and immediately rushed him to the same doctor that had treated Freddie. He took one look at him and said, 'I don't know how to say this, Florence, but I'm afraid he has the same thing.'

"We put him through the same tests at the Yale-New Haven Hospital and then took him to Johns Hopkins Metabolic Research Unit in Baltimore. Dr. Robert Cook operated on my Larry and found that where there should have been a brain there was only a round ball, an inert mass. When we put Larry

154

into the same hospital where his brother had died a few months before, life stopped for me....

"The doctors told us Larry wouldn't live long, but they were wrong. He lived to be 19 years old and died the same size he was when he was one year old. He never grew and was blind and deaf—nothing but a living vegetable for all those years."[2]

I must tell you that Florence and Fred Littauer eventually found Christ as Savior and overcame their terrible grief. Now their books and seminars are helping thousands of others find healing.

But think of their tragedy: one little brain-damaged boy dead at two years of age, and the other blind, deaf, and a living vegetable for 19 years, dying the same size he was at one year of age.

Seeing Ourselves as God Sees Us

If we could scan the pews and pulpits of churches and see beyond believers' adult-sized bodies into their stunted, dwarfed spirits fixated in various states of immaturity, as the heavenly Father sees them, could we endure it? If we ever caught a glimpse of our selfish, shriveled hearts, could we stand it?

Toddlers behind pulpits. Bewhiskered deacons sucking pacifiers. Colicky choir members clutching security blankets and demanding their own way. Gray-haired grandfathers struggling to learn their spiritual ABCs. Giggling, pimply-faced grandmothers. Fatigued leaders spoon-feeding pampered parishioners. Glowering businessmen, clutching their wallets and the keys to their Mercedes, pouting because they've been asked to share.

Pablum. Pampers. Potty training. It's enough to make the angels weep.

Entering the School of God's Spirit

A friend of mine who, after years of study, had just graduated from seminary with her doctorate, was given a special word from the Lord as she sat quietly worshiping in a Sunday morning service.

Although her eyes were closed, she suddenly saw a picture of a girl about eight or nine years of age wearing pigtails and a little plaid dress with a white collar, cradling her school books in one arm and waiting for the school bus. Instantly she recognized the little girl as herself, recalling having seen the exact photograph in one of her mother's old family picture albums.

Then the Lord spoke these words: "You have sat at the feet of men. Now I am enrolling you in the school of My Spirit, and you will be taught of the Lord."

I believe that is also God's word to many of us. God is calling us to lay aside our childish playthings and come and sit at His feet, for spiritual maturity is achieved not by striving after education, a ministry, or a position, but by longing after God and learning to linger in His presence.

If hungering after intimacy with God is this book's single most important lesson, then perhaps the second most important lesson is that personal character is crucial. Holy living is not optional. We've seen how God is shaking the Church today because leaders and laity have not taken seriously His command to "Be holy for I am holy." Mature believers are God-fearing believers.

Spirituality, morality, and unselfish service go hand in hand. Growing in Christ means growing in self-control. It means restraining the flesh's desire to indulge in sins such as lust, greed, and the pursuit of power. It means loving others enough to weep and intercede for their needs. It means guarding and guiding the younger ones in our midst by becoming spiritual mentors. It means overflowing celebration out of a pure heart. It means taking the starving by the hand and showing them where we have found bread.

A very real conflict is raging between the Kingdom of God and the kingdoms of this world. All around us stumble the bruised, the bleeding, and the broken. But warfare isn't kid stuff. Ministry isn't child's play.

It's time to let God pry our fingers away from the treasured playthings of the past, placing our chubby fingers in His strong hand. It's time to enroll in the school of God's Spirit and learn His will and His holy, wise ways. It's time to serve God's purpose in our generation. It's time to grow up!

Endnotes

1. Florence Littauer, *Blow Away the Black Clouds* (Eugene, Oregon: Harvest House Publishers, 1979, 1986), pp. 8-10.

2. Littauer, *Blow Away*, p. 8.

Also
by David Ravenhill

For those interested in contacting the author for speaking
engagements write to:

**David Ravenhill
Spikenard Ministries Ltd.
16858 Hwy 110 North
Lindale, TX   75771**

**Or call:
903-882-3942**

**Or FAX:
903-882-3740**

Foundationally Spirit-Filled. Biblically Sound. Spiritually Inspirational.

━━━ THE GOD CHASERS (National Best-selling Book)
by Tommy Tenney.

There are those so hungry, so desperate for His Presence, that they become consumed with finding Him. Their longing for Him moves them to do what they would otherwise never do: Chase God. But what does it really mean to chase God? Can He be "caught"? Is there an end to the thirsting of man's soul for Him? Meet Tommy Tenney—God chaser. Join him in his search for God. Follow him as he ignores the maze of religious tradition and finds himself, not chasing God, but to his utter amazement, caught by the One he had chased.

ISBN 0-7684-2016-4

━━━ ENCOUNTERING THE PRESENCE
by Colin Urquhart.

What is it about Jesus that, when we encounter Him, we are changed? When we encounter the Presence, we encounter the Truth, because Jesus is the Truth. Here Colin Urquhart, best-selling author and pastor in Sussex, England, explains how the Truth changes facts. Do you desire to become more like Jesus? The Truth will set you free!

ISBN 0-7684-2018-0

━━━ THE POWER OF BROKENNESS
by Don Nori.

Accepting Brokenness is a must for becoming a true vessel of the Lord, and is a stepping-stone to revival in our hearts, our homes, and our churches. Brokenness alone brings us to the wonderful revelation of how deep and great our Lord's mercy really is. Join this companion who leads us through the darkest of nights. Discover the *Power of Brokenness*.

ISBN 1-56043-178-4

━━━ AUDIENCE OF ONE
by Jeremy and Connie Sinnott.

More than just a book about worship, *Audience of One* will lead you into experiencing intimacy and love for the only One who matters—your heavenly Father. Worship leaders and associate pastors themselves, Jeremy and Connie Sinnott have been on a journey of discovering true spiritual worship for years. Then they found a whole new dimension to worship—its passion, intimacy, and love for the Father, your *audience of One*.

ISBN 0-7684-2014-8

Available at your local Christian bookstore.

Books to help you grow strong in Jesus

━━ CORPORATE ANOINTING

by Kelley Varner.

Just as a united front is more powerful in battle, so is the anointing when Christians come together in unity! In this classic book, senior pastor Kelley Varner of Praise Tabernacle in Richlands, North Carolina, presents a powerful teaching and revelation that will change your life! Learn how God longs to reveal the fullness of Christ in the fullness of His Body in power and glory.
ISBN 0-7684-2011-3

━━ DIGGING THE WELLS OF REVIVAL

by Lou Engle.

Did you know that just beneath your feet are deep wells of revival? God is calling us today to unstop the wells and reclaim the spiritual inheritance of our nation, declares Lou Engle. As part of the pastoral staff at Harvest Rock Church and founder of its "24-Hour House of Prayer," he has experienced firsthand the importance of knowing and praying over our spiritual heritage. Let's renew covenant with God, reclaim our glorious roots, and believe for the greatest revival the world has ever known!
ISBN 0-7684-2015-6

━━ THE HIDDEN POWER OF PRAYER AND FASTING

by Mahesh Chavda.

The praying believer is the confident believer. But the fasting believer is the overcoming believer. This is the believer who changes the circumstances and the world around him. He is the one who experiences the supernatural power of the risen Lord in his everyday life. An international evangelist and the senior pastor of All Nations Church in Charlotte, North Carolina, Mahesh Chavda has seen firsthand the power of God released through a lifestyle of prayer and fasting. Here he shares from decades of personal experience and scriptural study principles and practical tips about fasting and praying. This book will inspire you to tap into God's power and change your life, your city, and your nation!
ISBN 0-7684-2017-2

━━ THE LOST ART OF INTERCESSION

by Jim W. Goll.

Finally there is something that really explains what is happening to so many folk in the Body of Christ. What does it mean to carry the burden of the Lord? Where is it in Scripture and in history? Why do I feel as though God is groaning within me? No, you are not crazy; God is restoring genuine intercessory prayer in the hearts of those who are open to respond to His burden and His passion.
ISBN 1-56043-697-2

Available at your local Christian bookstore.

For more information and sample chapters, visit www.reapernet.com